MW00891378

CODING PUZZLES

Thinking in code
2nd Edition

@CODINGTMD

Dedicated to the memory of my dog,
Maomao,
who was passed away last year, aged 13.

Preface to the second edition

I made this book for fun at beginning, but I didn't expect I will get so many reponse from readers. It's really an interesting experience!

What this new edition brings to you:
1. Fix some typo in the first edition, reformat the code for readability, replace some graphs with high resolution images.
2. Add 32 new problems to fullfil the problem list. In the second edition, it contains 136 problems in Recursion, Divid and Conquer, Binary Search, Tree Traversal, Graph Traversal, Dynamic Programming, String Search etc, which is more than enough for preparing a software engineer interview. For each new problem, I add more details of the problem and algorithm analysis.
3. Add an Appendix in the end of this book for designing question preparation. This appendix includes some selected papers, books I had read in the past two years. And I think this is the most important change in the second edition. Learning what current industry does and keeping improving the design skill will help yourself in a long-term career.

Again, this book is used to present how to analysis a problem and link the inside the challenge with some existing algrithoms. The goal of this book is to improve the problem solving ability, not to be a collection of latest interview questions from Facebook, Google etc.

Hope this book can help you get your desired offer.
Good luck!

CodingTMD
@Seattle
Oct. 2014

Preface

If you are preparing the programming interview for a software engineer position, you might want to look at this book.

Make sure you have basic knowledge of data structure and algorithm, because this book is mostly focus on how to resolve the coding puzzles with existing data structure and algorithm. If you need some refresh of data structure and algorithm, there is a good book you might want to take a look first, <Introduction to Algorithms> by Thomas H. Cormen.

This book has 105 puzzles. Every puzzle contains a detailed explanation and some implementations. If you find any error in this book, please send your findings to codingtmd@outlook.com.

And at last, this book is only for fun, so that my friends can read it in their kindle offline. If you want to a free version, you can get it at http://fisherlei.blogspot.com/, but the prerequisite is you need to be able to understand Chinese☺

CodingTMD
@Seattle
Dec. 2013

Contents

*: the new added content in 2nd edition

*: the new added content in 2nd edition

*: the new added content in 2nd edition

*: the new added content in 2ⁿᵈ edition

1. 2 Sum

Given an array of integers, find two numbers such that they add up to a specific target number.
The function twoSum should return indices of the two numbers such that they add up to the target, where index1 must be less than index2. Please note that your returned answers (both index1 and index2) are not zero-based.
You may assume that each input would have exactly one solution.
Input: numbers={2, 7, 11, 15}, target=9
Output: index1=1, index2=2
» Solve this problem

[Thoughts]
There are three sorts of solutions:

The first solution is hashing.
Scan the array from the left to the right, and store the number and its index(the original index in the array) in the map. Then, scan the array again with the help of map. The time complexity is O(n).

The second solution is two-pointer scanning.
Sort the array first, unfortunately, you need to remember the original index during sorting. It's better to use a new object to hold the number-index mapping.After the array is sorted, then, use two pointers to scan from two bounds to the middle. Find the solution and return their original index. The time complexity is O(n*lgn).

> Note:
> **Two-pointers Scanning**
> *Two-pointer is a optimized way to search targets on top of a SORTED array. One pointer points to the head of the sorted array, and the other one points to the tail of the sorted array. The two points move towards the middle of the array until they meet.*

The third solution is brute-force searching.

This is the most obvious solution, but with the highest time complexity O(n*n)

[Code]
Following is the execution of solution 1 :

```
1:   vector<int> twoSum(vector<int> &numbers, int target) {
2:       map<int, int> mapping;
3:       vector<int> result;
4:       for(int i =0; i< numbers.size(); i++)
5:       {
6:           mapping[numbers[i]]=i;
7:       }
8:       for(int i =0; i< numbers.size(); i++)
9:       {
10:          int searched = target - numbers[i];
11:          if(mapping.find(searched) != mapping.end())
12:          {
13:              result.push_back(i+1);
14:              result.push_back(mapping[searched]+1);
15:              break;
16:          }
17:      }
18:      return result;
19:  }
```

Solution 2:

```
1:  struct Node
2:  {
3:      int val;
4:      int index;
5:      Node(int pVal, int pIndex):val(pVal), index(pIndex) {}
6:  };
7:  static bool compare(const Node &left, const Node &right)
8:  {
9:      return left.val < right.val;
10: }
```

```
11: vector<int> twoSum(vector<int> &numbers, int target) {
12:     vector<Node> elements;
13:     for(int i =0; i< numbers.size(); i++)
14:     {
15:         elements.push_back(Node(numbers[i], i));
16:     }
17:     std::sort(elements.begin(), elements.end(), compare);
18:     int start = 0, end = numbers.size()-1;
19:     vector<int> result;
20:     while(start < end)
21:     {
22:       int sum = elements[start].val + elements[end].val;
23:       if(sum == target)
24:       {
25:           result.push_back(elements[start].index+1);
26:           if(elements[start].index < elements[end].index)
27:             result.push_back(elements[end].index+1);
28:           else
29:             result.insert(result.begin(), elements[end].index+1);
30:           break;
31:       }
32:       else if(sum > target)
33:           end--;
34:       else
35:           start++;
36:     }
37:     return result;
38: }
```

Solution 3: two nested loop. The implementation of the solution is left out here.

Single Passed on leetcode

2. 3 Sum

Given an array S of n integers, are there elements a, b, c in S such that $a + b + c = 0$? Find all unique triplets in the array which gives the sum of zero.

Note:

- Elements in a triplet (a,b,c) must be in non-descending order. (ie, $a \le b \le c$)
- The solution set must not contain duplicate triplets.

```
For example, given array S = {-1 0 1 2 -1 -
4},

A solution set is:
(-1, 0, 1)
(-1, -1, 2)
```

» Solve this problem

[Thoughts]
Change the equation a little bit.

$$a + b + c = 0 \implies a + b = -c$$

So with the new equation, the problem is changed as finding two element a and b, which sums to –c.

Sort the array first. And use two pointers to scan from both sorted array bounds to middle. Since the problem requires no duplicate solution set. Need add some tricks to de-duplicate as below:

1. Line 19 ~ 24.
    filter the duplicate during two-pointer scanning. For example [-2, 0, 0, 2,2], the expected output should be [-2,0,2]. If no filter here, the output will be duplicate as [-2,0,2] and [-2,0,2]
2. Line 37
    filter the duplicate for outside iteration. For example [-2, -2, -2, 0,2].

[Code]

4

```
1:  vector<vector<int> > threeSum(vector<int> &num) {
2:      std::sort(num.begin(), num.end());
3:      vector<vector<int> > result;
4:      int len = num.size();
5:      for(int i =0; i< len; i++)
6:      {
7:          int target = 0-num[i];
8:          int start = i+1, end =len-1;
9:          while(start<end)
10:           {
11:               if(num[start] + num[end] == target)
12:               {
13:                   vector<int> solution;
14:                   solution.push_back(num[i]);
15:                   solution.push_back(num[start]);
16:                   solution.push_back(num[end]);
17:                   result.push_back(solution);
18:                   start++; end--;
19:                   while(start<end
20:                       && num[start] == num[start-1])
21:                       start++;
22:                   while(start<end
23:                       && num[end] == num[end+1])
24:                       end--;
25:               }
26:               else if(num[start] + num[end] < target)
27:               {
28:                   start++;
29:               }
30:               else
31:               {
32:                   end--;
33:               }
34:           }
35:       if(i<len-1)
```

```
36:          {
37:               while(num[i] == num[i+1]) i++;
38:          }
39:     }
40:     return result;
41: }
```

3. 3Sum Closest

Given an array *S* of *n* integers, find three integers in *S* such that the sum is closest to a given number, target. Return the sum of the three integers. You may assume that each input would have exactly one solution.

```
    For example, given array S = {-1 2 1 -4},
and target = 1.
    The sum that is closest to the target is 2.
(-1 + 2 + 1 = 2).
```

» Solve this problem

[Thoughts]
Similar as 3Sum. Only need to add a new variable to track the minimum history. See below highlight code for the differences.

[Code]
```
1:  int threeSumClosest(vector<int> &num, int target) {
2:      std::sort(num.begin(), num.end());
3:      int len = num.size();
4:      int minV = INT_MAX, record;
5:      for(int i =0; i< len; i++)
6:      {
7:          int start = i+1, end =len-1;
8:          while(start<end)
9:          {
10:             int sum = num[i] + num[start] + num[end];
11:             if(sum == target)
12:             {
13:                 minV = 0;
14:                 record = sum;
15:                 break;
16:             }
17:             if(sum < target)
```

```
18:            {
19:                if(target-sum < minV)
20:                {
21:                    minV = target-sum;
22:                    record = sum;
23:                }
24:                start++;
25:            }
26:            else
27:            {
28:                if(sum-target < minV)
29:                {
30:                    minV = sum - target;
31:                    record = sum;
32:                }
33:                end--;
34:            }
35:        }
36:        if(record == target) break;
37:        //de-duplicate
38:        while(i<len-1 && num[i] == num[i+1]) i++;
39:    }
40:    return record;
41: }
```

4. 4Sum

Given an array S of n integers, are there elements a, b, c, and d in S such that $a + b + c + d$ = target? Find all unique quadruplets in the array which gives the sum of target.
Note:

- Elements in a quadruplet (a,b,c,d) must be in non-descending order. (ie, $a \leq b \leq c \leq d$)
- The solution set must not contain duplicate quadruplets.

```
    For example, given array S = {1 0 -1 0 -2 2}, an
d target = 0.

    A solution set is:

    (-1,  0, 0, 1)

    (-2, -1, 1, 2)

    (-2,  0, 0, 2)
```

[Thoughts]
This problem is better understood after doing a little transformation:

$$a + b + c + d => (a+b) + (c+d).$$

Look at Problem "2 Sum". This problem can be done by doing "2 Sum" twice.

The first time, use two loops to calculate all the possible sums of the two numbers (a+b) and (c+d). For instance, using the above example S = {1 0 -1 0 -2 2}, and calculate all the possible two-number combinations S-Com and the mapping between S<->S-Com.
In this case, the S-Com = {-3, -2, -1, 0, 1, 2, 3}. And the mapping will be

S	S-Com
{-2,-1}	{-3}
{-2,0}	{-2}
{-2, 1}, {-1, 0}	{-1}

9

{0,0}, {-1, 1}, {-2,2}	{0}
{0, 1}, {-1,2}	{1}
{0, 2}	{2}
{1,2}	{3}

Then do a 2sum again based on S-Com.

Keep in mind that before returning all the results, filter the duplications. You should be able to finish this code by referring to previous "2Sum".

5. Add Binary

Giveng two binary strings, return their sum (also a binary string).
For example,
a = "11"
b = "1"
Return "100".
» Solve this problem

[Thoughts]
A general implementation. No trick here. Simulate the add process one digit by one. Don't miss the carry.

[Code]
```
1:   string addBinary(string a, string b) {
2:     int carry =0;
3:     string result;
4:     for(int i = a.size()-1, j = b.size()-1; i >=0 || j>=0; --i,--j)
5:     {
6:         int ai = i>=0? a[i]-'0':0;
7:         int bj = j>=0? b[j]-'0':0;
8:         int val = (ai+bj+carry)%2;
9:         carry = (ai+bj+carry) /2;
10:         result.insert(result.begin(), val+'0');
11:     }
12:     if(carry ==1)
13:     {
14:         result.insert(result.begin(), '1');
15:     }
16:     return result;
17:   }
```

[Note]
There is another extension. How to change the code to handle hexadecimal instead of binary. In this code, change the line 13 and line 14 from 2 to 16.

6. Add Two Numbers

You are given two linked lists representing two non-negative numbers. The digits are stored in reverse order and each of their nodes contain a single digit. Add the two numbers and return it as a linked list.

Input: (2 -> 4 -> 3) + (5 -> 6 -> 4)

Output: 7 -> 0 -> 8

» Solve this problem

[Thoughts]

Similar as "Add Binary". The logic part is same. And the only difference is the pointer operation because this is linked list.

[Code]

```
1:   ListNode *addTwoNumbers(ListNode *l1, ListNode *l2) {
2:       ListNode* result = new ListNode(-1);
3:       ListNode* pre = result;
4:       ListNode *pa = l1, *pb = l2;
5:       int carry =0;
6:       while(pa!=NULL || pb!=NULL)
7:       {
8:           int av = pa == NULL? 0:pa->val;
9:           int bv = pb == NULL? 0:pb->val;
10:          ListNode* node = new ListNode((av+bv+carry)%10);
11:          carry = (av+bv+carry)/10;
12:          pre->next = node;
13:          pre = pre->next;
14:          pa = pa==NULL? NULL:pa->next;
15:          pb = pb==NULL? NULL:pb->next;
16:      }
17:      if(carry >0)
18:          pre->next = new ListNode(1);
19:      pre = result->next;
20:      delete result;
21:      return pre;
```

```
22:    }
```

7. Anagrams

Given an array of strings, return all groups of strings that are anagrams.

Note: All inputs will be in lower-case.
» Solve this problem

[Thoughts]
Generate footprint for each string, if they has the same footprint, they are anagrams. But how to generate footprint is tricky. At beginning, I try to generate footprint as a full description of string content(as highlight code), but this costs too much time when the string is huge. Instead, I choose to generate hash number for each string.A potential risk is hash collision. So choose a prime number as the factor to avoid this.

[Code]

```
1:  vector<string> anagrams(vector<string> &strs) {
2:      vector<string> result;
3:      if(strs.size() ==0) return result;
4:      map<long, vector<string> > smap;
5:      for(int i =0; i< strs.size(); i++)
6:      {
7:          smap[footprint(strs[i])].push_back(strs[i]);
8:      }
9:      for(auto it = smap.begin(); it!=smap.end(); ++it)
10:     {
11:         if(it->second.size() <=1)
12:             continue;
13:         result.insert(result.begin(),
14:             it->second.begin(), it->second.end());
15:     }
16:     return result;
17: }
18: long footprint(string str)
19: {
20:     int index[26];
```

```
21:     memset(index, 0, 26*sizeof(int));
22:     for(int i = 0; i < str.size(); i++)
23:     {
24:         index[str[i]-'a']++;
25:     }
26:     /*string footp;
27:     for(int i =0; i<26; i++)
28:     {
29:         footp.append(1,i+'a');
30:         stringstream ss;
31:         ss << index[i];
32:         footp.append(ss.str());
33:     }*/
34:     long footp=0;
35:     int feed =7;
36:     for(int i =0; i< 26; i++)
37:     {
38:         footp= footp*feed +index[i];
39:     }
40:     return footp;
41: }
```

8. Best Time to Buy and Sell Stock

Say you have an array for which the ith element is the price of a given stock on day i.

If you were only permitted to complete at most one transaction (ie, buy one and sell one share of the stock), design an algorithm to find the maximum profit.

» Solve this problem

[Thoughts]

Scan the array from left to right. And keep tracking the minimal price in scanned elements. In the meantime, track the max profit by calculating the difference between current price and minimal price and updating the max profit if the difference is larger than existing max profit.

[Code]

```
1:   int maxProfit(vector<int> &prices) {
2:       // Start typing your C/C++ solution below
3:       // DO NOT write int main() function
4:       int minV=INT_MAX; int max =0;
5:       int diff=0;
6:       for(int i =0; i< prices.size(); i++)
7:       {
8:           if(prices[i]<minV) minV = prices[i];
9:           diff = prices[i] - minV;
10:          if(max<diff)
11:              max = diff;
12:      }
13:      return max;
14:  }
```

9. Best Time to Buy and Sell Stock II

Say you have an array for which the ith element is the price of a given stock on day i.
Design an algorithm to find the maximum profit. You may complete as many transactions as you like (ie, buy one and sell one share of the stock multiple times). However, you may not engage in multiple transactions at the same time (ie, you must sell the stock before you buy again).
» Solve this problem

[Thoughts]
A little different with previous one. Since we can make unlimited transactions, this question turns to sum all the positive price difference.

So, scan the array from left to right, and sum all positive diff value.

[Code]
```
1:   int maxProfit(vector<int> &prices) {
2:     // Start typing your C/C++ solution below
3:     // DO NOT write int main() function
4:     int max=0;
5:     int sum = 0;
6:     for(int i =1; i< prices.size(); i++)
7:     {
8:        int diff = prices[i] -prices[i-1];
9:        if(diff>0)
10:          sum+=diff;
11:    }
12:    return sum;
13:  }
```

10. Best Time to Buy and Sell Stock III

Say you have an array for which the ith element is the price of a given stock on day i.

Design an algorithm to find the maximum profit. You may complete at most *two* transactions.

Note:

You may not engage in multiple transactions at the same time (ie, you must sell the stock before you buy again).

» Solve this problem

[Thoughts]

One-dimension dynamic planning. Given an i, split the whole array into two parts:

[0,i] and [i+1, n], it generates two max value based on i, MaxProfit(0,i) and MaxProfit(i+1,n). So, we can define the transformation function as:

FinalMaxProfix = max(MaxProfit(0,i) + MaxProfit(i+1, n)) 0<=i<n

Pre-processing MaxProfit(0,i) and MaxProfit(i+1,n). And easy to find the FinalMaxProfit in one pass.

[Code]

Line 6~12 and Line 15~21 can be merged into one pass. But keep it for readability.

```
1:  int maxProfit(vector<int> &prices) {
2:      if(prices.size() <= 1) return 0;
3:      vector<int> maxFromLeft(prices.size(), 0);
4:      vector<int> maxFromRight(prices.size(), 0);
5:      int minV = INT_MAX, maxP = INT_MIN;
6:      for(int i =0; i< prices.size(); i++)
7:      {
8:          if(minV > prices[i]) minV = prices[i];
9:          int temp = prices[i] - minV;
10:         if(temp > maxP) maxP = temp;
```

```
11:        maxFromLeft[i] = maxP;
12:    }
13:    int maxV = INT_MIN;
14:    maxP = INT_MIN;
15:    for(int i =prices.size()-1; i>=0; i--)
16:    {
17:        if(maxV < prices[i]) maxV = prices[i];
18:        int temp = maxV - prices[i];
19:        if(temp > maxP) maxP = temp;
20:        maxFromRight[i] = maxP;
21:    }
22:    int maxProfit = INT_MIN;
23:    for(int i =0; i< prices.size()-1; i++)
24:    {
25:        int sum = maxFromLeft[i] + maxFromRight[i+1];
26:        if(sum > maxProfit) maxProfit = sum;
27:    }
28:    if(maxProfit < maxFromRight[0])
29:        maxProfit = maxFromRight[0];
30:    return maxProfit;
31: }
```

11. Balanced Binary Tree

Given a binary tree, determine if it is height-balanced.
For this problem, a height-balanced binary tree is defined as a binary tree in which the depth of the two subtrees of *every*node never differ by more than 1.
» Solve this problem

[Thoughts]
For the tree question, the most apparent way is to use Recursion. Here, for each node, check the left branch and right branch recursively.

[Code]

```
1:   bool isBalanced(TreeNode *root) {
2:     // Start typing your C/C++ solution below
3:     // DO NOT write int main() function
4:     if(root == NULL) return true;
5:     int val = GetBalance(root);
6:     if(val ==-1) return false;
7:     return true;
8:   }
9:   int GetBalance(TreeNode* node)
10: {
11:    if(node == NULL)
12:      return 0;
13:    int left = GetBalance(node->left);
14:    if(left == -1) return -1;
15:    int right = GetBalance(node->right);
16:    if(right == -1) return -1;
17:    if(left-right>1 || right-left>1)
18:      return -1;
19:    return left>right? left+1:right+1;
20: }
```

12. Binary Tree Preorder Traversal

Given a binary tree, return the *preorder* traversal of its nodes' values.
For example:
Given binary tree {1, #, 2, 3},

```
1
 \
  2
 /
3
```

return [1, 2, 3].
Note: Recursive solution is trivial, could you do it iteratively?

[Thoughts]
For tree traversal, the two normal ways are recursion and iteration.

If we take preorder as an example, the recursion solution is pretty straightforward:

```
visit node
for the visited node, recursively
        a. visit node->left
        b. visit node->right
```

And the recursion code is also brief,

```
preorder(node)
  if node == null then return
  visit(node)
  preorder(node.left)
  preorder(node.right)
```

But if we want to implement the traversal via iteration, we need to hire a extra stack/queue to maintain the visit sequence.

The pseudocode of iterative preorder traversal is as below.

```
iterativePreorder (node)
  parentStack = empty stack
  parentStack.push(null)
  top =  node
  while ( top != null )
      visit( top )
      if ( top.right ≠ null )
          parentStack.push(top.right)
      if ( top.left ≠ null )
          parentStack.push(top.left)
      top = parentStack.pop()
```

Besides preorder, there is same story for inorder and postorder traversal.
Attach the sample code for reference.

Inorder

```
inorder(node)
  if node == null then return
  inorder(node.left)
  visit(node)
  inorder(node.right)
```

```
iterativeInorder (node)
  parentStack = empty stack
  while (not parentStack.isEmpty() or node ≠
null)
      if (node ≠ null)
        parentStack.push(node)
        node = node.left
      else
        node = parentStack.pop()
        visit(node)
```

```
        node = node.right
```

Postorder

```
postorder(node)
  if node == null then return
  postorder(node.left)
  postorder(node.right)
  visit(node)
```

```
iterativePostorder(node)
  parentStack = empty stack
  lastnodevisited = null
  while (not parentStack.isEmpty() or node ≠
null)
    if (node ≠ null)
      parentStack.push(node)
      node = node.left
    else
      peeknode = parentStack.peek()
      if (peeknode.right ≠ null and
lastnodevisited ≠ peeknode.right)
        /* if right child exists AND
traversing node from left child, move right
*/
        node = peeknode.right
      else
        parentStack.pop()
        visit(peeknode)
        lastnodevisited = peeknode
```

[Code]

```
1:  vector<int> preorderTraversal(TreeNode *root) {
2:      stack<TreeNode*> tStack;
3:      vector<int> result;
4:      while(tStack.size()>0 || root != NULL)
5:      {
6:          if(root != NULL)
7:          {
8:              result.push_back(root->val);
9:              if(root->right !=NULL)
10:                 tStack.push(root->right);
11:             root = root->left;
12:         }
13:         else
14:         {
15:             root = tStack.top();
16:             tStack.pop();
17:         }
18:     }
19:     return result;
20: }
```

13. Binary Tree Inorder Traversal

Given a binary tree, return the *inorder* traversal of its nodes' values.
For example:
Given binary tree {1,#,2,3},

```
  1
   \
    2
   /
  3
```

return [1,3,2].
Note: Recursive solution is trivial, could you do it iteratively?
confused what "{1,#,2,3}" means? > read more on how binary tree is
serialized on OJ.
» Solve this problem

[Thoughts]
For recursion solution, it's very easy to write. But for iterative
solution, we need an extra stack to track the visited path.

[Code]
Recursion version

```
1:   vector<int> inorderTraversal(TreeNode *root) {
2:     // Start typing your C/C++ solution below
3:     // DO NOT write int main() function
4:     vector<int> result;
5:     inorderTra(root, result);
6:     return result;
7:   }
8:   void inorderTra(TreeNode* node, vector<int> &result)
9:   {
10:    if(node == NULL)
11:    {
12:      return;
```

```
13:    }
14:    inorderTra(node->left, result);
15:    result.push_back(node->val);
16:    inorderTra(node->right, result);
17:  }
```

Iteration version

```
1:   vector<int> inorderTraversal(TreeNode *root) {
2:     // Start typing your C/C++ solution below
3:     // DO NOT write int main() function
4:     vector<TreeNode*> sta;
5:     vector<int> result;
6:     if(root == NULL) return result;
7:     TreeNode* node =root;
8:     while(sta.size()>0 || node!=NULL)
9:     {
10:       while(node!=NULL)
11:       {
12:          sta.push_back(node);
13:          node = node->left;
14:       }
15:       node= sta.back();
16:       sta.pop_back();
17:       result.push_back(node->val);
18:       node =node->right;
19:     }
20:     return result;
21:   }
```

Note:
Post-order iteratively travel is bit tricky. Think about it.

14. Binary Tree Level Order Traversal

Given a binary tree, return the *level order* traversal of its nodes' values. (ie, from left to right, level by level).
For example:
Given binary tree {3,9,20,#,#,15,7},

```
     3
    / \
   9   20
      /  \
    15    7
```

return its level order traversal as:

```
[
  [3],
  [9,20],
  [15,7]
]
```

confused what "{1,#,2,3}" means? > read more on how binary tree is serialized on OJ. » Solve this problem

[Thoughts]

Two ways to resolve this problem:
1. Breadth first search
   Initial an int variable to track the node count in each level and print level by level. And here need a QUEUE as a helper.
2. Depth first search
   Rely on the recursion. Decrement level by one as you advance to the next level. When level equals 1, you've reached the given level and output them.
   The cons is, DFS will revisit the node, which make it less efficient than BFS. So normally, no one use DFS in this case.

[Code]

Here, only provide the BFS solution.

```
1:    vector<vector<int> > levelOrder(TreeNode *root) {
2:    vector<vector<int> > result;
3:    if(root == NULL) return result;
4:    queue<TreeNode*> nodeQ;
5:    nodeQ.push(root);
6:    int nextLevelCnt=0, currentLevelCnt=1;
7:    vector<int> layer;
8:    int visitedCnt=0;
9:    while(nodeQ.size() != 0)
10:   {
11:      TreeNode* node = nodeQ.front();
12:      nodeQ.pop();
13:      visitedCnt++;
14:      layer.push_back(node->val);
15:      if(node->left != NULL)
16:      {
17:        nodeQ.push(node->left);
18:        nextLevelCnt++;
19:      }
20:      if(node->right != NULL)
21:      {
22:        nodeQ.push(node->right);
23:        nextLevelCnt++;
24:      }
25:      if(visitedCnt == currentLevelCnt)
26:      {
27:        visitedCnt =0;
28:        currentLevelCnt = nextLevelCnt;
29:        nextLevelCnt=0;
30:        result.push_back(layer);
31:        layer.clear();
32:      }
33:   }
```

```
34:     return result;
35:  }
```

15.   Binary Tree Maximum Path Sum

Given a binary tree, find the maximum path sum.
The path may start and end at any node in the tree.
For example:
Given the below binary tree,

```
       1
      / \
     2   3
```

Return 6.
» Solve this problem

[Thoughts]
For each node like below example, there should be four paths existing for max path:

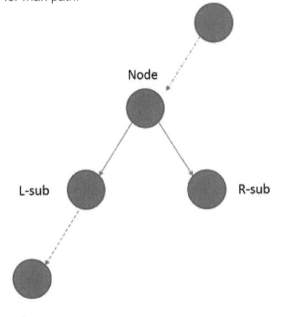

Node

L-sub   R-sub

1. Node only
2. L-sub + Node
3. R-sub + Node
4. L-sub + Node + R-sub

So, in the recursion process, keep tracing the four paths and pick up the max one in each step.

[Code]

```
1:   int maxPathSum(TreeNode *root) {
2:     // Start typing your C/C++ solution below
3:     // DO NOT write int main() function
4:     int maxAcrossRoot=INT_MIN;
5:     int maxEndByRoot = GetMax(root, maxAcrossRoot);
6:     return std::max(maxAcrossRoot, maxEndByRoot);
7:   }
8:   int GetMax(TreeNode *node, int& maxAcrossRoot)
9:   {
10:    if(node == NULL) return 0;
11:    int left = GetMax(node->left, maxAcrossRoot);
12:    int right = GetMax(node->right, maxAcrossRoot);
13:    int cMax = node->val;
14:    if(left>0)
15:      cMax+=left;
16:    if(right>0)
17:      cMax+=right;
18:    maxAcrossRoot = std::max(maxAcrossRoot, cMax);
19:    return std::max(
20:      node->val,
21:      std::max(node->val+left, node->val+right));
22:  }
```

16.   Climbing Stairs

You are climbing a stair case. It takes *n* steps to reach to the top. Each time you can either climb 1 or 2 steps. In how many distinct ways can you climb to the top?
» Solve this problem

[Thoughts]
A transformation of Fibonacci Number.
(http://en.wikipedia.org/wiki/Fibonacci_number)

Solve it by one dimension dynamic programming. The transition function should be:

$f(n)$	$=$	$f(n-1)$	$+$	$f(n-2)$	$n>2$;
or	$=$	1			$n=1$
or	$=$	2			$n=2$

[Code]
```
1:   int climbStairs(int n) {
2:     // Start typing your C/C++ solution below
3:     // DO NOT write int main() function
4:     int fn_2 =1, fn_1=2;
5:     if(n==1) return fn_2;
6:     if(n ==2) return fn_1;
7:     int fn;
8:     for(int i =3; i<=n; i++)
9:     {
10:       fn = fn_2+fn_1;
11:       fn_2 = fn_1;
12:       fn_1= fn;
13:     }
14:     return fn;
15:   }
```

17.   Clone Graph

Clone an undirected graph. Each node in the graph contains
a `label` and a list of its `neighbors`.

Nodes are labeled uniquely. We use # as a separator for each
node, and , as a separator for node label and each neighbor of
the node. As an example, consider the serialized
graph `{0,1,2#1,2#2,2}`.

The graph has a total of three nodes, and therefore contains
three parts as separated by #.

1.   First node is labeled as 0. Connect node 0 to both
     nodes 1 and 2.

2.   Second node is labeled as 1. Connect node 1 to node 2.

3.   Third node is labeled as 2. Connect node 2 to node 2 (itself),
     thus forming a self-cycle.

Visually, the graph looks like the following:

```
     1
   / \
  /   \
 0 --- 2
     / \
     \_/
```

[Thoughts]
In the Coding Puzzles I, there is a similar problem to "copy list
with random pointer".

In previous solution, we can generate a duplicate list by iterating
the list multiple times for copying nodes, linking copied nodes
and splitting the copies list out of original one.

Here, we can still use the same conception to solve the problem.
But here we don't want to use a while loop to keep iterating the
graph, instead, we introduce extra space usage for tracking the
mapping between the original node and copied node. With this
relationship mapping, we can link the copied nodes in the same
pass when we do the DFS in the graph.

[Code]

```
1:  /**
2:   * Definition for undirected graph.
3:   * struct UndirectedGraphNode {
4:   *   int label;
5:   *   vector<UndirectedGraphNode *> neighbors;
6:   *   UndirectedGraphNode(int x) : label(x) {};
7:   * };
8:   */
9:  UndirectedGraphNode *cloneGraph(
10:       UndirectedGraphNode *node)
11:  {
12:      if(node == NULL) return NULL;
13:      unordered_map<UndirectedGraphNode *,
14:              UndirectedGraphNode *> nodeMap;
15:      queue<UndirectedGraphNode *> visit;
16:      visit.push(node);
17:      UndirectedGraphNode * nodeCopy =
18:              new UndirectedGraphNode(node->label);
19:      nodeMap[node] = nodeCopy;
20:      while (visit.size()>0)
21:      {
22:          UndirectedGraphNode * cur = visit.front();
23:          visit.pop();
24:          for (int i = 0; i< cur->neighbors.size(); ++i)
25:          {
26:              UndirectedGraphNode * neighb =
27:                  cur->neighbors[i];
28:              if (nodeMap.find(neighb) == nodeMap.end())
29:              {
30:                  // no copy of neighbor node yet.
31:                  // create one and link it with the copy of cur
32:                  UndirectedGraphNode* neighbCopy =
```

```
33:                new UndirectedGraphNode(neighb->label);
34:                nodeMap[cur]->neighbors.push_back(
35:                    neighbCopy);
36:                nodeMap[neighb] = neighbCopy;
37:                visit.push(neighb);
38:            }
39:            else
40:            {
41:                // already a copy there.
42:                // Link it with the copy of cur
43:                nodeMap[cur]->neighbors.push_back(
44:                    nodeMap[neighb]);
45:            }
46:        }
47:    }
48:    return nodeCopy;
49: }
```

18.   Combination Sum

Given a set of candidate numbers (**C**) and a target number (**T**), find all unique combinations in **C** where the candidate numbers sums to **T**.

The **same** repeated number may be chosen from **C** unlimited number of times.

Note:

- All numbers (including target) will be positive integers.
- Elements in a combination (a1, a2, $\cdots$, ak) must be in non-descending order. (ie, a1 $\leq$ a2 $\leq \cdots \leq$ ak).
- The solution set must not contain duplicate combinations.

For example, given candidate set 2,3,6,7 and target 7,

A solution set is:

[7]

[2, 2, 3]

» Solve this problem

[Thoughts]

This is a classic recursion question. For each candidate, add its value and verify whether equals to he target. If it hit, add it as a part of solution.

[Code]

```
1:  vector<vector<int> > combinationSum(
2:      vector<int> &candidates, int target)
3:  {
4:      vector<vector<int> > result;
5:      vector<int> solution;
6:      int sum=0;
7:      std::sort(candidates.begin(), candidates.end());
8:      GetCombinations(
9:          candidates,sum, 0, target, solution, result);
10:     return result;
11: }
```

```
12:  void GetCombinations(
13:      vector<int>& candidates,
14:      int& sum,
15:      int level,
16:      int target,
17:      vector<int>& solution,
18:      vector<vector<int> >& result)
19:  {
20:      if(sum > target) return;
21:      if(sum == target)
22:      {
23:          result.push_back(solution);
24:          return;
25:      }
26:      for(int i =level; i< candidates.size(); i++)
27:      {
28:          sum+=candidates[i];
29:          solution.push_back(candidates[i]);
30:          GetCombinations(
31:              candidates, sum, i, target, solution, result);
32:          solution.pop_back(); // do not miss cleaning the num
33:          sum-=candidates[i];
34:      }
35:  }
```

19. Combination Sum II

Given a collection of candidate numbers (**C**) and a target number (**T**), find all unique combinations in **C** where the candidate numbers sums to **T**.

Each number in **C** may only be used **once** in the combination.

Note:

- • All numbers (including target) will be positive integers.
- • Elements in a combination (a1, a2, ⋯ , ak) must be in non-descending order. (ie, a1 ≤ a2 ≤ ⋯ ≤ ak).
- • The solution set must not contain duplicate combinations.

For example, given candidate set 10,1,2,7,6,1,5 and target 8,

A solution set is:

```
[1, 7]
[1, 2, 5]
[2, 6]
[1, 1, 6]
```

» Solve this problem

[Thoughts]

Similar with previous "Combination Sum". But the only difference is about how to handle the index and skip duplicate candidate. See the special logic highlighted in red.

[Code]

```
1:  vector<vector<int> > combinationSum2(
2:      vector<int> &num, int target)
3:  {
4:      vector<vector<int> > result;
5:      vector<int> solution;
6:      int sum=0;
7:      std::sort(num.begin(), num.end());
8:      GetCombinations(num,sum, 0, target, solution, result);
9:      return result;
```

```
10: }
11:
12: void GetCombinations(
13:     vector<int>& candidates,
14:     int& sum,
15:     int level,
16:     int target,
17:     vector<int>& solution,
18:     vector<vector<int> >& result)
19: {
20:     if(sum > target) return;
21:     if(sum == target)
22:     {
23:         result.push_back(solution);
24:         return;
25:     }
26:     for(int i =level; i< candidates.size(); i++)
27:     {
28:         sum+=candidates[i];
29:         solution.push_back(candidates[i]);
30:         GetCombinations(
31:             candidates, sum, i+1, target, solution, result);
32:         solution.pop_back();
33:         sum-=candidates[i];
34:         while( i<candidates.size()-1
35:             && candidates[i] == candidates[i+1])
36:             i++;
37:     }
38: }
```

20. Combinations

Given two integers *n* and *k*, return all possible combinations of *k* numbers out of 1 ... *n*.
For example,
If *n* = 4 and *k* = 2, a solution is:

```
[
    [2,4],
    [3,4],
    [2,3],
    [1,2],
    [1,3],
    [1,4],
]
```

» Solve this problem

[Thoughts]
Similar as previous "Conbination Sum". But here the terminate condition is "k", not sum. In code, the difference is about the termination condition. See highlight code.

[Code]
```
1:   vector<vector<int> > combine(int n, int k) {
2:       // Start typing your C/C++ solution below
3:       // DO NOT write int main() function
4:       vector<vector<int> > result;
5:       vector<int> solution;
6:       GetCombine(n,k,1, solution, result);
7:       return result;
8:   }
9:   void GetCombine(
10:      int n,
11:      int k,
12:      int level,
13:      vector<int>& solution,
14:      vector<vector<int> >& result)
```

```
15:    {
16:      if(solution.size() == k)
17:      {
18:        result.push_back(solution);
19:        return;
20:      }
21:      for(int i =level; i<= n; i++)
22:      {
23:        solution.push_back(i);
24:        GetCombine(n,k,i+1, solution, result);
25:        solution.pop_back();
26:      }
27:    }
```

21.   Construct Binary Tree from Preorder and Inorder Traversal

Given preorder and inorder traversal of a tree, construct the binary tree.
Note:
You may assume that duplicates do not exist in the tree.
» Solve this problem

[Thoughts]

Let's see some example first.

```
_____7_____
      /              \
   __10__          __2
   /    \          /
  4      3        _8
          \      /
          1    11
```

The preorder and inorder traversals for the binary tree above is:

```
preorder = {7,10,4,3,1,2,8,11}
inorder = {4,10,3,1,7,11,8,2}
```

The first node in preorder always the **root of the tree**. We can break the tree like:
1st round:
preorder: {7}, {10,4,3,1}, {2,8,11}
inorder: {4,10,3,1}, {7}, {11, 8,2}

```
      _____7_____
      /                 \
{4,10,3,1}         {11,8,2}
```

Since we already find that {7} will be the root, and in "inorder" traversals, all the data in the left of {7} will construct the left sub-tree. And the right part will construct a right sub-tree. We can the left and right part agin based on the preorder.

2nd round

left part	right part
preorder: {10}, {4}, {3,1}	{2}, {8,11}
inorder: {4}, {10},	{11,8}, {2}

```
 _____7_____
 /                      \
 __10__                 __2
/      \                /
4      {3,1}         {11,8}
```

see that, {10} will be the root of left-sub-tree and {2} will be the root of right-sub-tree.

Same way to split {3,1} and {11,8}, yo will get the complete tree now.

```
 _____7_____
 /                      \
 __10__                 __2
/      \                /
4      3              _8
        \            /
         1          11
```

So, simulate this process from bottom to top with recursion as following code.

[Code]

```
1:  TreeNode *buildTree(
2:     vector<int> &preorder,
3:     vector<int> &inorder)
4:  {
5:     return BuildTreePI( preorder, inorder,
6:         0, preorder.size()-1, 0, preorder.size());
7:  }
8:  TreeNode* BuildTreePI(
9:     vector<int> &preorder,
10:    vector<int> &inorder,
11:    int p_s, int p_e,
12:    int i_s, int i_e)
13: {
14:    if(p_s > p_e)
15:       return NULL;
16:    int pivot = preorder[i_s];
17:    int i =p_s;
18:    for(;i< p_e; i++)
19:    {
20:       if(inorder[i] == pivot)
21:          break;
22:    }
23:    TreeNode* node = new TreeNode(pivot);
24:    node->left = BuildTreePI(preorder, inorder,
25:          p_s, i-1, i_s+1, i-p_s+i_s);
26:    node->right = BuildTreePI(preorder, inorder,
27:          i+1, p_e, i-p_s+i_s+1, i_e);
28:    return node;
29: }
```

22.   Container With Most Water

Given n non-negative integers a_1, a_2, ..., a_n, where each represents a point at coordinate (i, a_i). n vertical lines are drawn such that the two endpoints of line i is at (i, a_i) and $(i, 0)$. Find two lines, which together with x-axis forms a container, such that the container contains the most water.

Note: You may not slant the container.

» Solve this problem

[Thoughts]

Think a while and still no idea? This problem is actually challenge! Let's bring in a hint here.

> **For any container, its volume depends on the shortest board.**

Get the idea? The solution is actually quite simple. Two-pointer scanning. And always move the pointer with shorter board. The next max will only happen when you try to change the shorter board!

[Code]

```
1:   int maxArea(vector<int> &height) {
2:      // Start typing your C/C++ solution below
3:      // DO NOT write int main() function
4:      int start =0;
5:      int end = height.size()-1;
6:      int maxV = INT_MIN;
7:      while(start<end)
8:      {
9:         int contain = min(height[end], height[start]) * (end-start);
10:        maxV = max(maxV, contain);
11:        if(height[start]<= height[end])
12:        {
13:           start++;
14:        }
15:        else
```

```
16:    {
17:      end--;
18:    }
19:  }
20:  return maxV;
21: }
```

23. Convert Sorted Array to Binary Search Tree

Given an array where elements are sorted in ascending order, convert it to a height balanced BST.
» Solve this problem

[Thoughts]
If we build BST from array, we can build it from top to bottom, like
1. choose the middle one as root,
2. build left sub BST via left part array
3. build right sub BST via right part array
4. do this recursively.

[Code]
```
1:      TreeNode *sortedArrayToBST(vector<int> &num) {
2:          return BuildTree(num, 0, num.size()-1);
3:      }
4:      TreeNode *BuildTree(vector<int> &num, int start, int end)
5:      {
6:          if(start>end) return NULL;
7:          if(start == end) return new TreeNode(num[start]);
8:          int mid = (start+end)/2;
9:          TreeNode *node = new TreeNode(num[mid]);
10:         node->left = BuildTree(num, start, mid-1);
11:         node->right = BuildTree(num, mid+1, end);
12:         return node;
13:     }
```

24. Convert Sorted List to Binary Search Tree

Given a singly linked list where elements are sorted in ascending order, convert it to a height balanced BST.
» Solve this problem

[Thoughts]
It is similar with "**Convert Sorted Array to Binary Search Tree**". But the difference here is we have no way to random access item in O(1), because it is linked list.

If we build BST from array, we can build it from top to bottom, like
1. choose the middle one as root,
2. build left sub BST
3. build right sub BST
4. do this recursively.

But for linked list, we can't do that because Top-To-Bottom are heavily relied on the index operation.
As an alternative solution, we can use Bottom-TO-Top:
> 1. Get the length of list first
> 2. Travel the tree in-order and populate the tree node. The bottom-up approach enables us to access the list in its order while creating nodes.

With this, we no longer need to find the middle element.

[Code]
```
1:  TreeNode *sortedListToBST(ListNode *head) {
2:      int len =0;
3:      ListNode *p = head;
4:      while(p)
5:      {
6:          len++;
7:          p = p->next;
8:      }
9:      return BuildBST(head, 0, len-1);
10: }
```

```
11:
12:  TreeNode* BuildBST(ListNode*& list, int start, int end)
13:  {
14:      if (start > end) return NULL;
15:      int mid = (start+end)/2;
16:      TreeNode *leftChild = BuildBST(list, start, mid-1);
17:      TreeNode *parent = new TreeNode(list->val);
18:      parent->left = leftChild;
19:      list = list->next;
20:      parent->right = BuildBST(list, mid+1, end);
21:      return parent;
22:  }
23:
```

25. Copy List with Random Pointer

A linked list is given such that each node contains an additional random pointer which could point to any node in the list or null.

Return a deep copy of the list.

[Thoughts]
In this problem, the deep copy not only copies the node value, but also need to keep the random link relationship in the new list.

We can solve it in 3 steps as below figure:
1. Traverse the list. For each node N, make a duplication N'. And insert the N' after N.
2. Traverse the list again. For each original node N, duplicate the random pointer in N'. If N->random points to M, set N'->random pointing to M'.
3. Splite the copied nodes out of the list and get the expected result.

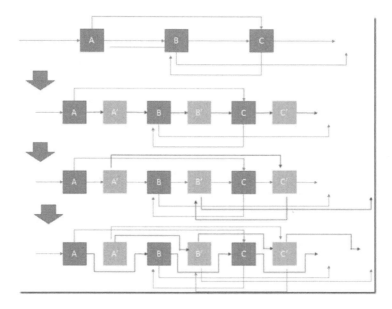

[Code]

```
1:  RandomListNode *copyRandomList(RandomListNode *head) {
2:      //insert nodes
3:      RandomListNode * cur = head;
4:      while(cur!=NULL)
5:      {
6:          RandomListNode* temp = new RandomListNode(cur->label);
7:          temp->next = cur->next;
8:          cur->next = temp;
9:          cur = temp->next;
10:     }
11:     // copy random pointer
12:     cur = head;
13:     while(cur != NULL)
14:     {
15:         RandomListNode* temp = cur->next;
16:         if(cur->random != NULL)
17:             temp->random = cur->random->next;
18:         cur = temp->next;
19:     }
20:     //decouple two links
21:     cur = head;
22:     RandomListNode* dup = head == NULL? NULL:head->next;
23:     while(cur != NULL)
24:     {
25:         RandomListNode* temp = cur->next;
26:         cur->next = temp->next;
27:         if(temp->next!=NULL)
28:             temp->next = temp->next->next;
29:         cur = cur->next;
30:     }
31:     return dup;
32: }
```

26. Count and Say

The count-and-say sequence is the sequence of integers beginning as follows:
1, 11, 21, 1211, 111221, ...
1 is read off as "one 1" or 11.
11 is read off as "two 1s" or 21.
21 is read off as "one 2, then one 1" or 1211.
Given an integer *n*, generate the *n*th sequence.
Note: The sequence of integers will be represented as a string.
» Solve this problem

[Thoughts]
No trick here. Only some string operations. The only beautiful thing is Line9. seq[seq.size()] always '\0'. It will help to save an "if" statement.

[Code]
```
1:   string countAndSay(int n) {
2:     string seq = "1";
3:     int it = 1;
4:     while(it<n)
5:     {
6:       stringstream newSeq;
7:       char last = seq[0];
8:       int count =0;
9:       for(int i =0; i<= seq.size();i++)
10:      {
11:        if(seq[i] ==last)
12:        {
13:          count ++;
14:          continue;
15:        }
16:        else
17:        {
18:          newSeq<<count<<last;
19:          last = seq[i];
```

```
20:          count =1;
21:        }
22:      }
23:      seq = newSeq.str();
24:      it++;
25:    }
26:    return seq;
27: }
```

27.   Decode Ways

A message containing letters from A-Z is being encoded to numbers using the following mapping:

```
'A' -> 1
'B' -> 2
...
'Z' -> 26
```

Given an encoded message containing digits, determine the total number of ways to decode it.

For example,

Given encoded message "12", it could be decoded as "AB" (1 2) or "L" (12).

The number of ways decoding "12" is 2.

» Solve this problem

[Thoughts]

Similar as previous "Climbing Stairs". DP. Just add some logic to compare character.

Transformation function can be defined as:

Count[i]	=	Count[i-1]		if S[i-1] is a valid char
	or =	Count[i-1]	+ Count[i-2]	if S[i-1]
and S[i-2] together is still a valid char.				

[Code]

```
1:   int numDecodings(string s) {
2:     if(s.empty() || s[0] =='0') return 0;
3:     if(s.size() ==1) return check(s[0]);
4:     int fn=0, fn_1=0, fn_2=1;
5:     fn_1 = (check(s[0]) * check(s[1]))+check(s[0], s[1]);
6:     for(int i=2; i< s.size(); i++)
7:     {
8:        if(check(s[i])) fn+= fn_1;
9:        if(check(s[i-1], s[i])) fn+=fn_2;
10:       if(fn ==0)
```

```
11:       return 0;
12:     fn_2 = fn_1;
13:     fn_1 = fn;
14:     fn=0;
15:   }
16:   return fn_1;
17: }
18: int check(char one)
19: {
20:   return (one != '0') ? 1 : 0;
21: }
22: int check(char one, char two)
23: {
24:   return (one == '1' || (one == '2' && two <= '6'))? 1 : 0;
25: }
```

28.   Distinct Subsequences

Given a string **S** and a string **T**, count the number of distinct subsequences of **T** in **S**.

A subsequence of a string is a new string which is formed from the original string by deleting some (can be none) of the characters without disturbing the relative positions of the remaining characters. (ie, "ACE" is a subsequence of "ABCDE"while "AEC" is not).

Here is an example:

S = "rabbbit", **T** = "rabbit"

Return 3.

» Solve this problem

[Thoughts]

DP again. The key is how to get the transition function. Let's define t[i][j] as the number of dictinct subsequences of T[0,i] in S[0,j]

If the last character in T[0,i] not equals the last character in S[0,j], that is, T[i] != S[j], the t[i][j] is exactly same as t[i][j-1].

But if they are equal, that is T[i] == S[j], there are two possibilities:

- Don't use S[j] to match. The count of distinct subsequences of T[0,i] in S[0,j-1]
- Use S[j] to match. The count of distinct subsequences of T[0,i-1] in S[0,j-1]

So t[i][j] = t[i][j-1] + t[i-1][j-1]

The transition function is

t[i][j]	=	t[i][j-1]	if T[i] != S[j]	
	or =	t[i][j-1] +	t[i-1][j-1]	if T[i] == S[j]

[Code]

```
1:  int numDistinct(string S, string T) {
2:      // Start typing your C/C++ solution below
3:      // DO NOT write int main() function
4:      int match[200];
5:      if(S.size() < T.size()) return 0;
6:      match[0] = 1;
```

```
7:     for(int i=1; i <= T.size(); i++)
8:       match[i] = 0;
9:     for(int i=1; i<= S.size(); i ++)
10:      for(int j =T.size(); j>=1; j--)
11:        if(S[i-1] == T[j-1])
12:          match[j]+= match[j-1];
13:      return match[T.size()];
14:  }
```

29. Divide Two Integers

Divide two integers without using multiplication, division and mod operator.

[Thoughts]
Bit operation. The main idea is to simulate the division by

1. rotating the divisor to the left(<<1) until finding the number which is most close to dividend.
2. Substract the dividend by the rotated divisor and get the difference as the new dividend.
3. Repeat doing #1 and #2 until dividend is zero

[Code]
```
1:  int divide(int dividend, int divisor) {
2:    // Start typing your C/C++ solution below
3:    // DO NOT write int main() function
4:    int sign = 1;
5:    if(dividend ==0) return 0;
6:    if(dividend <0) sign*=-1;
7:    if(divisor <0) sign *=-1;
8:    unsigned int dvd = dividend >0? dividend: -dividend;
9:    unsigned int dvs = divisor >0? divisor: -divisor;//abs(divisor);
10:   unsigned int inc[32];
11:   unsigned int migValue = dvs;
12:   int i =0;
13:   while(migValue > 0 && migValue <= dvd)
14:   {
15:     inc[i] = migValue;
16:     migValue = migValue <<1;
17:     i++;
18:   }
19:   i--;
20:   unsigned int res = 0;
21:   while(i>=0 && dvd!=0)
22:   {
```

```
23:      if(dvd >= inc[i])
24:      {
25:        dvd = dvd - inc[i];
26:        res += 1<<i;
27:      }
28:      i--;
29:    }
30:    res*= sign;
31:    return res;
32:  }
```

30. Edit Distance

Given two words word1 and word2, find the minimum number of steps required to convert word1 to word2. (each operation is counted as 1 step.)
You have the following 3 operations permitted on a word:
a) Insert a character
b) Delete a character
c) Replace a character
» Solve this problem

[Thoughts]
This is an interesting problem. This is a two-dimension dynamic programming.

Define d(i,j) as the edit distance of A[0, i] and B[0, j]. If assume A[0, i] as somestr1c and B[0, j] as somestr2d, we can get following assumption too:

- The edit distance of "somestr1" and "somestr2" is d(i-1,j-1)
- The edit distance of "somestr1" and "somestr2" is d(i,j-1)
- The edit distance of "somestr1" and "somestr2d" is d(i-1,j)

Based on these three variable, we can derive the d(i,j) as :

- If c==d, it is obvious that d(i,j) is same as d(i-1,j-1)
- If c!=d, let's see how to convert,
  - If replace c with d, the edit distance is the one converting "somestr1" to "somestr2" plus 1, that is, d(i-1,j-1) + 1
  - if append d after c, the edit distance is the one converting "somestr1c" to "somestr2" plus , that is, d(i,j-1) + 1
  - if delete c, the edit distance is the one converting "somestr1" to "somestr2d", that is, d(i-1,j) + 1

  After comaring the 3 edit distances, pick up the minimal one as the solution.

So, the transition function is here:

```
dp[i][j]       =      dp[i-1][j-1]     if  (A[i]  ==
B[j])
```

```
        or =    min(dp[i][j-1], dp[i-1][j],
                dp[i-1][j-1]) +1; if A[i] !=
B[j]
        or =    j  if i ==0
        or =    i  if j ==0
```

[Code]

No need to initialize a two-dimension array to represent d[i,j].
Here, use two iterative arrays.

```
1:  int minDistance(string word1, string word2) {
2:      int * matchUp = new int[20000];
3:      int* matchDown = new int[20000];
4:      for(int i=0; i<= smallStr.size(); i++)
5:      {
6:          matchUp[i] = 0;
7:          matchDown[i] = i;
8:      }
9:      for(int i=1; i<=word1.size(); i++)
10:     {
11:         matchUp[0] = i;
12:         for(int j= 1; j<=word2.size(); j++)
13:         {
14:             if(word1[i-1] == word2[j-1])
15:             {
16:                 matchUp[j] = matchDown[j-1];
17:             }
18:             else
19:             {
20:                 matchUp[j] = min(matchDown[j], matchDown[j-1]);
21:                 matchUp[j] = min(matchUp[j], matchUp[j-1]) +1;
22:             }
23:         }
24:         int* temp = matchUp;
25:         matchUp = matchDown;
26:         matchDown = temp;
27:     }
```

```
28:    return matchDown[word2.size()];
29: }
```

31. Evaluate Reverse Polish Notation

Evaluate the value of an arithmetic expression in Reverse Polish Notation.
Valid operators are +, -, *, /. Each operand may be an integer or another expression.
Some examples:
```
["2", "1", "+", "3", "*"] -> ((2 + 1) * 3) -> 9
["4", "13", "5", "/", "+"]->(4 + (13 / 5))-> 6
```

[Thoughts]
Usually, stack is the best match for solving reverse polish notation.
For this question, we need to introduce a stack here and process the expression one character by one.

> *If current char is a number, push it into stack*
> *If current char is an operator, pop two elements out. Calculate the result and push back to stack.*

And in the end, the left number in the stack is the result.

[Code]
```
1: int evalRPN(vector<string> &tokens) {
2:    stack<int> operand;
3:    for(int i =0; i< tokens.size(); i++)
4:    {
5:        if ((tokens[i][0] == '-' && tokens[i].size()>1)
6:            || (tokens[i][0] >= '0' && tokens[i][0] <= '9'))
7:        {
8:            operand.push(atoi(tokens[i].c_str()));
9:            continue;
10:       }
11:       int op1 = operand.top();
12:       operand.pop();
13:       int op2 = operand.top();
14:       operand.pop();
15:       if(tokens[i] == "+") operand.push(op2+op1);
16:       if(tokens[i] == "-") operand.push(op2-op1);
17:       if(tokens[i] == "*") operand.push(op2*op1);
18:       if(tokens[i] == "/") operand.push(op2/op1);
19:    }
20:    return operand.top();
21: }
```

32. First Missing Positive

Given an unsorted integer array, find the first missing positive integer.
For example,
Given [1,2,0] return 3,
and [3,4,-1,1] return 2.
Your algorithm should run in $O(n)$ time and uses constant space.
» Solve this problem

[Thoughts]
If there is a unlimited array C here, we can use counting sort. Like for each A[i], set C[A[i]] =1. After iterating array A, iterate array C and return the first element which is zero.

But unfortunately, only constant space is available. In this case, reuse array A.
Maintain A as a sorted array, during the iteration, for each A[i],
        If A[i] != i, keep swapping A[i] and A[A[i]], until either A[i] == A[A[i]] or no element availale to

Then, go through array A again, and find the first element which not meet A[i] ==i condition.

[Code]
In the real implementation, there is a little trick. Since problem asked for positive number, so, no need to store zero. A[0] should be used to store number 1 instead of 0. The equation below used is A[i] == i+1, not A[i] == i. See the highlight part for this trick.

```
1:   int firstMissingPositive(int A[], int n) {
2:     // Start typing your C/C++ solution below
3:     // DO NOT write int main() function
4:     int i =0;
5:     for(int i =0; i< n; i++)
6:     {
7:       while(A[i] != i+1)
8:       {
```

```
9:        if(A[i] <= 0 || A[i] >n || A[i] == A[A[i] -1]) break;
10:       int temp = A[i];
11:       A[i] = A[temp-1];
12:       A[temp-1] = temp;
13:     }
14:   }
15:   for(int i =0; i< n; i++)
16:    if(A[i]!=i+1)
17:      return i+1;
18:    return n+1;
19: }
```

33.   Flatten Binary Tree to Linked List

Given a binary tree, flatten it to a linked list in-place.
For example,
Given

The flattened tree should look like:

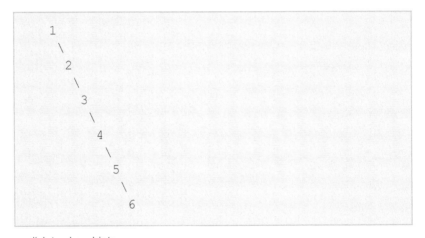

click to show hints.
» Solve this problem

[Thoughts]
Flatten the tree in recursion. For each node K,

1. Flatten the left sub-tree to a linked list A
2. Insert node K to the linked list A and as the new head
3. Flatten the right sub-tree to a linked list B, and append B to the end of A.

[Code]

```
1:    void flatten(TreeNode *root) {
2:        if(root == NULL) return;
3:        TreeNode* right = root->right;
4:        if(lastVisitedNode != NULL)
5:        {
6:            lastVisitedNode->left = NULL;
7:            lastVisitedNode->right = root;
8:        }
9:        lastVisitedNode = root;
10:       flatten(root->left);
11:       flatten(right);
12:   }
```

[Extension]

If change the problem to ask for an **in-order** flattening, how to solve it?

pre-order is simple because the root always is the head of flatten list. But if flatten the tree with in-order sequence, need extra parameter to track the head and tail of each flattened sun-tree. For example, below binary tree.

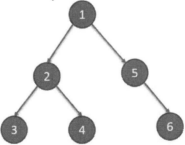

If we flatten it with in-order, the process should like below. And here I use the left pointer of head node to track the tail node.

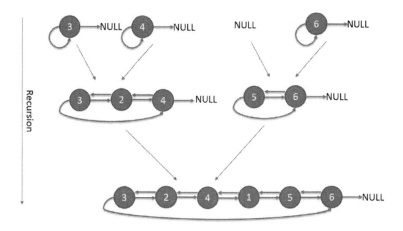

```
1:   TreeNode* flatten(TreeNode *root) {
2:     if (root == NULL) return NULL;
3:     TreeNode* rightTree = root->right;
4:     TreeNode* newHead = root;
5:     TreeNode* leftList = flatten(root->left);
6:     if (leftList != NULL)
7:     {
8:        newHead = leftList;
9:        TreeNode* tail = leftList->left;
10:       tail->right = root;
11:       root->left = tail;
12:       leftList->left = root;
13:    }
14:    TreeNode* rightList = flatten(rightTree);
15:    if (rightList != NULL)
16:    {
17:       root->right = rightList;
18:       newHead->left = rightList->left;
19:       rightList->left = root;
20:    }
21:    return newHead;
22: }
```

34. Gas Station

There are *N* gas stations along a circular route, where the amount of gas at station *i* is gas[i].

You have a car with an unlimited gas tank and it costs cost[i] of gas to travel from station *i* to its next station (*i*+1). You begin the journey with an empty tank at one of the gas stations.

Return the starting gas station's index if you can travel around the circuit once, otherwise return -1.

Note:
The solution is guaranteed to be unique.

[Thoughts]
Let's start from the most obvious way to target this proble. If we pick any station from the circular as the start station, it's east to calculate the left gas amount after travesering the whole circular. Sp, it needs O(n) to decide whether each station S_i is the expected start station or not. In order to find the start index, we need to apply the same above logic on every node until there is one station which fits the conditions. The overall complexity will be O(n) * O(n) =: O(n²).

But no one will propose this problem and expect only the most trivial solution. Could we solve it in O(n) and one pass iteration?

Think about the problem ""Let's analysis it a little bit deep. Actually, for each station, we only care the change of the amount in the gas tank.

Define diff[i] as the amount change of gas in the ith station. We can get:

```
diff[i] = gas[i] - cost[i]   0<=i <n
```

And thie problem could be decomposed into two questions:
1.   Does this circular exist a solution?
2.   If yes, where is the start index?

For the question #1, it's easy. We only need to sum up all the diff value, like leftGas = $\sum$diff[i]. If the leftGas is positive, it means there must be at least one solution in the circular. If the leftGas is negative, it means no such index existing. (Think why?) It needs O(n) to get the leftGas value.

For the question #2, where is the start index? Assume we take a sub range [i, j] (i< j) from the circular.
Define

```
sum[i,j] = ∑diff[k] where i<=k<j
```

If sum[i, j] < 0, the start index won't be in range [i,j](the same reason as question #1). For example, assume there is a solution and T is the start index in circular [0, n]. then we know for any k (0<=k<T-1), the sum[k, T-1] must be a negative number, otherwise, the start index should be k. And same, sum[T, n] must be larger than 0, otherwise, the start index won't be T, instead it should be some station between T and n. So, in order to solve question #2, we only need to find the first positive continuous sub range in the circular

And one more thing, both question #1 and question #2 could be addressed in one iteration.

[Code]

```
1: int canCompleteCircuit(vector<int> &gas, vector<int> &cost) {
2:     vector<int> diff(gas.size());
3:     for(int i =0; i< gas.size(); ++i)
4:     {
5:         diff[i] = gas[i] - cost[i];
6:     }
7:     int leftGas=0, sum =0, startnode=0;
8:     for(int i =0; i<gas.size(); ++i)
9:     {
10:        leftGas += diff[i];
11:        sum += diff[i];
12:        if(sum <0) //if less than 0, skip it
```

```
13:        {
14:            startnode = i+1;
15:            sum=0;
16:        }
17:    }
18:    if(leftGas <0)
19:    return -1;
20:    else
21:    return startnode;
22: }
```

35. Generate Parentheses

Given *n* pairs of parentheses, write a function to generate all combinations of well-formed parentheses.
For example, given *n* = 3, a solution set is:
"((()))", "(()())", "(())()", "()(())", "()()()"
» Solve this problem

[Thoughts]
Build it in recursion,
        If the count of left parenthses is less than n, can append more left parenthses;
        If the count of right parenthses is less than the left one, can append more right parenthses.

[Code]
```
1:  void CombinationPar(vector<string>& result, string& sample,
2:      int deep, int n, int leftNum, int rightNum)
3:  {
4:      if(deep == 2*n)
5:      {
6:          result.push_back(sample);
7:          return;
8:      }
9:      if(leftNum<n)
10:     {
11:         sample.push_back('(');
12:         CombinationPar(
13:             result, sample, deep+1, n, leftNum+1, rightNum);
14:         sample.resize(sample.size()-1);
15:     }
16:     if(rightNum<leftNum)
17:     {
18:         sample.push_back(')');
19:         CombinationPar(
20:             result, sample, deep+1, n, leftNum, rightNum+1);
21:         sample.resize(sample.size()-1);
```

```
22:    }
23: }
24:
25: vector<string> generateParenthesis(int n) {
26:     vector<string> result;
27:     string sample;
28:     if(n!= 0)
29:         CombinationPar(result, sample, 0, n, 0, 0);
30:     return result;
31: }
32:
```

36. Gray Code

The gray code is a binary numeral system where two successive values differ in only one bit.
Given a non-negative integer *n* representing the total number of bits in the code, print the sequence of gray code. A gray code sequence must begin with 0.
For example, given *n* = 2, return [0,1,3,2]. Its gray code sequence is:

```
00 - 0
01 - 1
11 - 3
10 - 2
```

Note:
For a given *n*, a gray code sequence is not uniquely defined.
For example, [0,2,3,1] is also a valid gray code sequence according to the above definition.
For now, the judge is able to judge based on one instance of gray code sequence. Sorry about that.
» Solve this problem

[Thoughts]
look more example when n=3
```
000
001
011
010
110
111
101
100
```

And the pattern comes out. The gray code of n=k, is the reverse sequence of the gray code of n=k-1 plus 1<<k.

[Code]
```
1:  vector<int> grayCode(int n) {
2:    // Start typing your C/C++ solution below
```

```
3:     // DO NOT write int main() function
4:     vector<int> result;
5:     result.push_back(0);
6:     for(int i=0; i< n; i++)
7:     {
8:       int highestBit = 1<<i;
9:       int len = result.size();
10:       for(int i = len-1; i>=0; i--)
11:       {
12:         result.push_back(highestBit + result[i]);
13:       }
14:     }
15:     return result;
16:   }
```

And since gray code is a muture encoding protocol used in the industry, there is also a math solution.

```
1:  vector<int> grayCode(int n)
2:  {
3:     vector<int> ret;
4:     int size = 1 << n;
5:     for(int i = 0; i < size; ++i)
6:       ret.push_back((i >> 1)^i);
7:     return ret;
8:  }
```

37. Implement strStr()

Implement strStr().
Returns a pointer to the first occurrence of needle in haystack,
or **null** if needle is not part of haystack.
» Solve this problem

[Thoughts]
It's easy to implement a O(n^2) solution by comparing the needle
with every substring in the haystack, as code example #1. But a
beauty solution is to use KMP, which provides a O(n) solution in
average. But KMP need to pre-process the string for recognizing
pattern.

[Code]

```
1:    char *strStr(char *haystack, char *needle) {
2:      // Start typing your C/C++ solution below
3:      // DO NOT write int main() function
4:      if(haystack == NULL || needle == NULL)
5:        return NULL;
6:      int hLen = strlen(haystack);
7:      int nLen = strlen(needle);
8:      if(hLen<nLen)
9:      return NULL;
10:     for(int i=0; i<hLen - nLen+1; i++)
11:     {
12:       int j=0;
13:       char* p = &haystack[i];
14:       for(; j< nLen; j++)
15:       {
16:           if(*p != needle[j])
17:               break;
18:           p++;
19:       }
20:       if(j == nLen)
```

```
21:      return &haystack[i];
22:   }
23:   return NULL;
24: }
```

But the most efficient way of implementing strStr() is to use KMP algorithm. If not familiar with KMP, search the wiki.

```
1:  char *strStr(char *haystack, char *needle) {
2:     if(haystack == NULL || needle == NULL) return NULL;
3:     int hlen = strlen(haystack);
4:     int nlen = strlen(needle);
5:     if(nlen ==0) return haystack;
6:     if(hlen == 0 ) return NULL;
7:     int pattern[100000];
8:     GeneratePattern(needle, nlen, pattern);
9:     return Match(haystack, needle, pattern);
10: }
11:
12: void GeneratePattern(char* str, int len, int* pattern)
13: {
14:    pattern[0] = -1;
15:    int k =-1;
16:    for(int j =1; j< len; j++)
17:    {
18:       while(k >-1 && str[k+1] != str[j])
19:          k = pattern[k];
20:       if(str[k+1] == str[j])
21:          k++;
22:       pattern[j] = k;
23:    }
24: }
25:
26: char* Match(char* haystack, char* needle, int* pattern)
27: {
```

```
28:    int hlen = strlen(haystack);
29:    int nlen = strlen(needle);
30:    int k =-1;
31:    for(int j =0; j< hlen; j++, haystack++)
32:    {
33:        while(k >-1 && needle[k+1] != *haystack)
34:            k = pattern[k];
35:        if(needle[k+1] == *haystack)
36:            k++;
37:        if(k == nlen-1)
38:            return haystack-k;
39:    }
40:    return NULL;
41: }
```

38. Insert Interval

Given a set of *non-overlapping* intervals, insert a new interval into the intervals (merge if necessary).
You may assume that the intervals were initially sorted according to their start times.
Example 1:
Given intervals [1,3],[6,9], insert and merge [2,5] in as [1,5],[6,9].
Example 2:
Given [1,2],[3,5],[6,7],[8,10],[12,16], insert and merge [4,9] in as [1,2],[3,10],[12,16].
This is because the new interval [4,9] overlaps with [3,5],[6,7],[8,10].
» Solve this problem

[Thoughts]
Iterate the interval one by one,
        If the new interval's end is less than current interval's start, insert the new interval here
        If the new interval has overlap with current interval, merge two intervals together as the new interval for next inserting.

[Code]
```
1:  vector<Interval> insert(
2:      vector<Interval> &intervals, Interval newInterval)
3:  {
4:      vector<Interval>::iterator it = intervals.begin();
5:      while(it!= intervals.end())
6:      {
7:          if(newInterval.end < it->start)
8:          {
9:              intervals.insert(it, newInterval);
10:             return intervals;
11:         }
12:         else if(newInterval.start > it->end)
13:         {
```

```
14:              it++;
15:              continue;
16:          }
17:      else
18:          {
19:              newInterval.start =
20:                  min(newInterval.start, it->start);
21:              newInterval.end =
22:                  max(newInterval.end, it->end);
23:              it =intervals.erase(it);
24:          }
25:      }
26:      intervals.insert(intervals.end(), newInterval);
27:      return intervals;
28: }
29:
```

[More challenge]
If the intervals are distributed in a ring, and currently give you a new interval, how could you insert the interval to the ring? For example, if the ring is [0,255], and there is a interval [1,234] in the ring, currently insert a new interval [222,4], what's the result? The result should [1,4]! And you can see lots of tricky cases in the boundary.

The solution is simple, actually, if the interval across 0, split into two parts and merge them in the ring seperatelly. For example, if given an interval [234,7] to insert, split this interval to two [234,255], [0,7] and insert them one by one. And at the end, check the head element and tail element, if they are linked, merge them together.

39. Integer to Roman

Given an integer, convert it to a roman numeral.
Input is guaranteed to be within the range from 1 to 3999.
» Solve this problem

[Thoughts]
An implementation problem. The challenge is how to handle the
digit conversion in different partition range:
- 1<=digit <=3
- digit =4
- digit = 5
- 5<digit<=8
- digit =9

[Code]
```
1:  string intToRoman(int num) {
2:      char symbol[7] = { 'I','V','X', 'L','C', 'D','M'};
3:      string roman;
4:      int scale = 1000;
5:      for(int i =6; i>=0; i-=2)
6:      {
7:          int digit = num/scale;
8:          if(digit != 0)
9:          {
10:             if(digit <= 3)
11:             {
12:                 roman.append(digit, symbol[i]);
13:             }
14:             else if(digit ==4)
15:             {
16:                 roman.append(1, symbol[i]);
17:                 roman.append(1, symbol[i+1]);
18:             }
19:             else if(digit ==5)
20:             {
21:                 roman.append(1, symbol[i+1]);
```

```
22:            }
23:            else if(digit <=8)
24:            {
25:                roman.append(1, symbol[i+1]);
26:                roman.append(digit-5, symbol[i]);
27:            }
28:            else if(digit ==9)
29:            {
30:                roman.append(1, symbol[i]);
31:                roman.append(1, symbol[i+2]);
32:            }
33:        }
34:        num = num%scale;
35:        scale/=10;
36:    }
37:    return roman;
38: }
```

40. Interleaving String

Given *s1*, *s2*, *s3*, find whether *s3* is formed by the interleaving of *s1* and *s2*.
For example,
Given:
s1 = "aabcc",
s2 = "dbbca",
When *s3* = "aadbbcbcac", return true.
When *s3* = "aadbbbaccc", return false.
» Solve this problem

[Thoughts]
Could we do this via merge sort like below?

```
1:  bool isInterleave(string s1, string s2, string s3) {
2:      if(s3.size() != (s1.size() + s2.size()))
3:      {
4:          return false;
5:      }
6:      int i =0, j= 0, k=0;
7:      while(i< s1.size() && j< s2.size())
8:      {
9:          if(s1[i] == s3[k])
10:         {
11:             i ++;
12:         }
13:         else if(s2[j] == s3[k])
14:         {
15:             j++;
16:         }
17:         else
18:         {
19:             return false;
20:         }
21:         k++;
22:     }
```

```
23:    while(i< s1.size())
24:    {
25:      if(s1[i] == s3[k])
26:      {
27:         i++;k++;
28:      }
29:      else
30:      {
31:         return false;
32:      }
33:    }
34:    while(j<s2.size())
35:    {
36:      if(s2[j] == s3[k])
37:      {
38:         j++;k++;
39:      }
40:      else
41:      {
42:         return false;
43:      }
44:    }
45:    return true;
46: }
47:
```

The answer is NO. Because merge sort didn't conside the combination of S1 and S2. For example, {"C","CA", "CAC"}.

This is still a dynamic programming problem. Let's define the S1, S2, and S3 as below:

$$s1 = a1, a2 ....a(i-1), ai$$
$$s2 = b1, b2, ...b(j-1), bj$$
$$s3 = c1, c3, ...c(i+j-1), c(i+j)$$

Define match[i][j] as S1[0, i] and S2[0,j] matches S3[0, (i+j)].

If ai == c(i+j), we know match[i][j] = match[i-1][j]. see below example.

> *s1 = a1, a2 ....a(i-1)*
> *s2 = b1, b2, ...b(j-1), bj*
> *s3 = c1, c3, ...c(i+j-1)*

The same as, if bj == c(i+j), match[i][j] = match[i][j-1].
So, the transition function shoule be:

```
Match[i][j]

    =   (s3.lastChar == s1.lastChar) && Match[i-1][j]

        ||(s3.lastChar == s2.lastChar) && Match[i][j-1]

Initia conditions:

    i=0 && j=0, Match[0][0] = true;

    i=0,  s3[j] = s2[j], Match[0][j] |= Match[0][j-1]

          s3[j] != s2[j], Match[0][j] = false;

    j=0,  s3[i] = s1[i], Match[i][0] |= Match[i-1][0]

          s3[i] != s1[i], Match[i][0] = false;
```

[Code]

```
1:  bool isInterleave(string s1, string s2, string s3) {
2:
3:      bool *matchUp = new bool[s2.size() +1];
4:      bool *matchDown = new bool[s2.size()+1];
5:      if(s3.size() != (s1.size() + s2.size())) return false;
6:      //initialize
7:      matchDown[0] = true;
8:      for(int i =1; i< s2.size() +1; i++)
9:      {
10:         if(s2[i-1] == s3[i-1])
11:             matchDown[i] |= matchDown[i-1];
12:         else
13:             matchDown[i]= false;
```

```
14:     }
15:     matchUp[0] = true;
16:     for(int i =1; i< s1.size() +1; i++)
17:     {
18:         if(s1[i-1] == s3[i-1])
19:             matchUp[0] |= matchDown[0];
20:         else
21:             matchUp[0]= false;
22:         for(int j =1;j<s2.size() +1; j++)
23:         {
24:             matchUp[j]=false;
25:             if(s1[i-1] == s3[i+j-1])
26:             {
27:                 matchUp[j] |= matchDown[j];
28:             }
29:             if(s2[j-1] == s3[i+j-1])
30:             {
31:                 matchUp[j] |= matchUp[j-1];
32:             }
33:         }
34:         bool* temp = matchUp;
35:         matchUp = matchDown;
36:         matchDown = temp;
37:     }
38:     delete matchup;
39:     delete matchDown;
40:     return matchDown[s2.size()];
41: }
42:
```

41. Jump Game

Given an array of non-negative integers, you are initially
positioned at the first index of the array.
Each element in the array represents your maximum jump length
at that position.
Determine if you are able to reach the last index.
For example:
A = [2,3,1,1,4], return true.
A = [3,2,1,0,4], return false.
» Solve this problem

[Thoughts]
One- dimension dynamic programming. If define jump[i] as the
max left steps when jumps from 0 to I, the transition function can
be derived as below

```
jump[i] = max(jump[i-1], A[i-1]) -1, i!=0
        = 0 , i==0
```

So scan the array from left to right, and try to find any i that leads
to "jump[i]<0". If this i exists, it means the robot won't be able to
arrive i and return false. Otherwise, means robot can arrive the
end of array, return true.

[Code]
```
1:  bool canJump(int A[], int n) {
2:      int* jump = new int[n];
3:      jump[0] = 0;
4:      for(int i=1; i < n; i++)
5:      {
6:          jump[i] = max(jump[i-1], A[i-1]) -1;
7:          if(jump[i] <0)
8:              return false;;
9:      }
10:     return jump[n-1] >=0;
11: }
```

And here, we can also make another optimization. Do we really need an array(jump[]) to track the steps? The answer is NO. We can also use one variable to track the maximal right boundary this robot can reach. And update this variable during the scanning. If the variable already reaches the end of the array, return true.

```
1:    bool canJump(int A[], int n) {
2:        int maxCover = 0;
3:        for(int start =0; start<= maxCover && start<n; start++)
4:        {
5:            if(A[start]+start > maxCover)
6:                maxCover = A[start]+start;
7:            if(maxCover >= n-1) return true;
8:        }
9:        return false;
10:   }
```

42. Jump Game II

Given an array of non-negative integers, you are initially positioned at the first index of the array.
Each element in the array represents your maximum jump length at that position.
Your goal is to reach the last index in the minimum number of jumps.
For example:
Given array A = [2,3,1,1,4]
The minimum number of jumps to reach the last index is 2.
(Jump 1 step from index 0 to 1, then 3 steps to the last index.)
» Solve this problem

[Thoughts]
Greedy search. Scan the integer array from left to right, for each element, calculate the max right boundary it can reach(A[i] + i).

In the implementation, can use a dynamic window to track the search range. Update the range index after each round scanning.

[Code]
```
1:  int jump(int A[], int n) {
2:      int start = 0;
3:      int end = 0;
4:      int count =0;
5:      if(n == 1) return 0;
6:      while(end < n)
7:      {
8:          int max = 0;
9:          count++;
10:         for(int i =start; i<= end ; i++ )
11:         {
12:             if(A[i]+i >= n-1)
13:             {
14:                 return count;
15:             }
```

```
16:            if(A[i]+ i > max)
17:                max = A[i]+i;
18:        }
19:        start = end+1;
20:        end = max;
21:    }
22: }
23:
```

43. Largest Rectangle in Histogram

Given *n* non-negative integers representing the histogram's bar height where the width of each bar is 1, find the area of largest rectangle in the histogram.

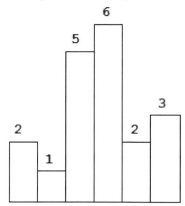

Above is a histogram where width of each bar is 1, given height = [2,1,5,6,2,3].

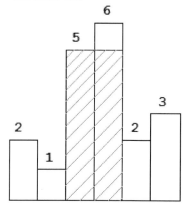

The largest rectangle is shown in the shaded area, which has area = 10 unit.

For example,

Given height = [2,1,5,6,2,3],

return 10.

» Solve this problem

[Thoughts]

Really good problem. The most straight forward solution is, scan the height value from left to right, and for each height scanned, iterate all the previous height to calculate the rectangle, and track the maximal value. The time complexity is O(n^2).

```
1:  int largestRectangleArea(vector<int> &height) {
2:      int maxV = 0;
3:      for(int i =0; i< height.size(); i++)
4:      {
5:          int minV = height[i];
6:          for(int j =i; j>=0; j--)
7:          {
8:              minV = std::min(minV, height[j]);
9:              int area = minV*(i-j+1);
10:             if(area > maxV)
11:                 maxV = area;
12:         }
13:     }
14:     return maxV;
15: }
```

As you see, previous code contains a lot of duplicate computation. Not every height value worths an iteration. A small improvement is, only trigger the calculation when there is a peak. See below red code.

```
1:  int largestRectangleArea(vector<int> &height) {
2:      int maxV = 0;
3:      for(int i =0; i< height.size(); i++)
4:      {
5:          if(i+1 < height.size() &&
6:              height[i] <= height[i+1]) // if not peak node, skip it
7:              continue;
8:          int minV = height[i];
9:          for(int j =i; j>=0; j--)
10:         {
```

```
11:            minV = std::min(minV, height[j]);
12:            int area = minV*(i-j+1);
13:            if(area > maxV)
14:            maxV = area;
15:        }
16:    }
17:    return maxV;
18: }
```

So, for a O(n^2) solution, we are done. But, could we do better? Yes, there is also a O(n) solution.

As showed in below figure, look at Height #4(the red dotted line), which is less than previous Height #3 and #2. When we process Height #4, we know it doesn't need to maintain Height #2 and #3 anymore, because in later part, there won't be any rectangle which can make use of #2 and #3. In this case, we can eliminate the diff part (black) and combine #2, #3 and #4 together as a new rectangle for later processing.

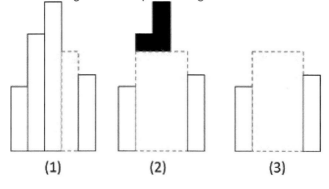

(1)   (2)   (3)

Here, the solution comes out. Open a stack which holds the element in increasing order. Each time, compare the processing height with current height with the top element of stack and keep doing this until the top element is less than current height. One trick here is, at the end, we need to push a zero into the stack to kick the merge process with all the elements in the stack.the top of stack. If the current height is larger than the top element of stack, push the current height into stack as the new top.

Otherwise, merge the

```
1:  int largestRectangleArea(vector<int> &h) {
2:      stack<int> S;
3:      h.push_back(0); // the last trigger
4:      int sum = 0;
5:      for (int i = 0; i < h.size(); i++) {
6:          if (S.empty() || h[i] > h[S.top()]) S.push(i);
7:          else {
8:              int tmp = S.top();
9:              S.pop();
10:             sum = max(sum, h[tmp]*(S.empty()? i : i-S.top()-1));
11:             i--;
12:         }
13:     }
14:     return sum;
15: }
```

44. Length of Last Word

Given a string *s* consists of upper/lower-case alphabets and empty space characters ' ', return the length of last word in the string.
If the last word does not exist, return 0.
Note: A word is defined as a character sequence consists of non-space characters only.
For example,
Given *s* = "Hello World",
return 5.
» Solve this problem

[Thoughts]
An interesting implementation problem. There are 4 possibilities of the last word as below (* stands for zero or more empty spaces)
1. "*"
2. "*word"
3. "*word*"
4. "word*"

So the algorithm is, scan the string from back to front. Skip all empty spaces at the end and capture the first word.

[Code]
```
1:  int lengthOfLastWord(const char *s) {
2:      int len = strlen(s);
3:      if( len== 0) return 0;
4:      int i = len-1;
5:      while(s[i] == ' ' && i>=0) i--;
6:      if(i == -1)
7:      {
8:          return 0;
9:      }
10:     int end = i;
11:     for(; i >=0; i--)
12:     {
```

```
13:        if(s[i] == ' ')
14:            break;
15:    }
16:    if(i ==-1)
17:        return end+1;
18:    return end-i;
19: }
```

The previous code is good. But not beauty enough. It can also be implemented as below

```
1:    int lengthOfLastWord(const char *s) {
2:        int len = strlen(s);
3:        int count = 0;
4:        for(int i =len-1; i>=0; i--)
5:        {
6:            if(s[i] == ' ')
7:            {
8:                if(count ==0) continue;
9:                else return count;
10:           }
11:           count++;
12:        }
13:        return count;
14:    }
```

45. Letter Combinations of a Phone Number

Given a digit string, return all possible letter combinations that the number could represent.
A mapping of digit to letters (just like on the telephone buttons) is given below.

Input: Digit string "23"

Output: ["ad", "ae", "af", "bd", "be", "bf", "cd", "ce", "cf"].

Note:
Although the above answer is in lexicographical order, your answer could be in any order you want.
» Solve this problem

[Thoughts]
A classical recursion problem. Similar as permutation.

[Code]
```
1:  vector<string> letterCombinations(string digits) {
2:      string trans[] = {"", " ", "abc", "def", "ghi", "jkl",
3:          "mno", "pqrs", "tuv", "wxyz"};
4:      vector<string> set;
5:      string seq;
6:      Generater(trans, digits, 0, seq, set);
7:      return set;
8:  }
9:  void Generater(string trans[], string& digits,
```

```
10:  int deep, string& result, vector<string>& set)
11:  {
12:      if(deep -- digits.size())
13:      {
14:          set.push_back(result);
15:          return;
16:      }
17:
18:      // convert ACSII code to integer
19:      int curDig = digits[deep] - 48;
20:      for(int i =0; i < trans[curDig].size(); i++)
21:      {
22:          result.push_back(trans[curDig][i]);
23:          Generater(trans, digits, deep+1, result, set);
24:          result.resize(result.size() -1);
25:      }
26:  }
```

46. Linked List Cycle

Given a linked list, determine if it has a cycle in it.

Follow up:
Can you solve it without using extra space?

[Thoughts]
Interesting problem. But need to think it divergently.

Here we can still use two pointers, P_{slow} and P_{fast}. For P_{slow}, each time it moves only one step, but for P_{fast}, each time it moves two steps. If there is a cycle in the linked list, P_{slow} and P_{fast} will definitely meet. Otherwise, no cycle.

[Code]
```
1:  bool hasCycle(ListNode *head) {
2:      if(head == NULL) return false;
3:      ListNode* first = head;
4:      ListNode* second = head->next;
5:      while(first != NULL && second != NULL)
6:      {
7:          if(first == second) return true;
8:          first = first->next;
9:          second = second->next;
10:         if(second == NULL)
11:             return false;
12:         second = second->next;
13:     }
14:     return false;
15: }
```

47. Linked List Cycle II

Given a linked list, return the node where the cycle begins. If there is no cycle, return `null`.

Follow up:
Can you solve it without using extra space?

[Thoughts]
Before we moved to the delicate solution, let's review the most trivial way first. Definitely, we can use the solution of "Linked List Cycle" to check whether there is a cycle in the list. If there is, we can traverse the list again. For each visited node, check whether this node is in the cycle or not. And return the first node in the cycle as the solution. The time complexity is $O(n^2)$.

Now, let's look at this problem from mathematic perspective. Assume there is a cycle in the list as below. The length of the cycle is Y and the length of the left part of list is X.

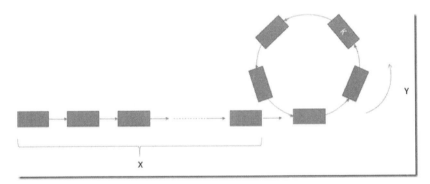

Suppose, there are two pointers, P_{slow} and P_{fast}. For P_{slow}, each time it moves only one step, but for P_{fast}, each time it moves two steps. If they meet with each other at Node K after t moves, we can get

```
For Pslow, it moves following steps:
    t = X + nY + K  ①
For Pfast, it moves following steps:
    2t = X + mY + K  ②
m,n are unknown variables
```

If we use equation ① to replace the t in the equation ②, we can get

$$2X + 2nY + 2K = X + mY + K$$
$$\Rightarrow \quad X+K = (m-2n)Y \quad ③$$

And now, we know X and K are complementary based on Y. In this particular problem, it means after two pointers meet with each other, moving another X steps will arrive the **head** node of cycle. This solution is only O(n) complexity.

[Code]

```
1:  ListNode *detectCycle(ListNode *head) {
2:      ListNode * first = head;
3:      ListNode * second = head;
4:      while(first != NULL && second != NULL)
5:      {
6:          first = first->next;
7:          second = second->next;
8:          if(second != NULL)
9:          second = second->next;
10:          if(first == second)
11:          break;
12:      }
13:      if(second == NULL) return NULL;
14:      // move for another X steps to find the head
15:      first = head;
16:      while(first!=second)
17:      {
18:          first = first->next;
19:          second = second->next;
20:      }
21:      return second;
22: }
```

48. Longest Common Prefix

Write a function to find the longest common prefix string amongst an array of strings.
» Solve this problem

[Thoughts]
An implementation problem. Add character to prefix one by one. And for each character, compare it with all strings. If it matches all the strings, add it to prefix. If not, break and return exsiting prefix as the longest one.

[Code]
```
1:    string longestCommonPrefix(vector<string> &strs) {
2:        string prefix;
3:        if(strs.size() ==0) return prefix;
4:        int len =0;
5:        while(1)
6:        {
7:            char var;
8:            int i=0;
9:            for(; i< strs.size(); i++)
10:           {
11:               if(i ==0) var =strs[0][len];
12:               if(strs[i].size() == len || var != strs[i][len])
13:               break;
14:           }
15:           if(i!= strs.size())
16:               break;
17:           len++;
18:           prefix.append(1, var);
19:       }
20:       return prefix;
21:    }
```

49. Longest Consecutive Sequence

Given an unsorted array of integers, find the length of the longest consecutive elements sequence.

For example,

Given [100, 4, 200, 1, 3, 2],

The longest consecutive elements sequence is [1, 2, 3, 4].

Return its length: 4.

Your algorithm should run in O(*n*) complexity.
» Solve this problem

[Thoughts]
For each num, define D[num] as the longest consecutive sequence from k to num, 0<k<num

So D[num] = D[num-1] +1   if num-1 in the map
       =0   if num-1 not in the map

But unfortunately, the unordered_map doesn't keep any order of sequence. It's hard to do the DP via a loop.

Here can use Memorization to optimize the code. So that for each fresh node, it only visits once. It is O(n) code.

And in the code , the second 'for' loop and the third 'for' loop could be merged together, but here keep them separated for readability.

[Code]
```
1:  int longestConsecutive(vector<int> &num) {
2:      unordered_map<int, int> hashmap;
3:      vector<int> length(num.size(),0);
4:      for(int i =0; i< num.size(); i++)
5:      {
6:          hashmap[num[i]]=i;
7:      }
8:      for(int i =0; i< num.size(); i++)
```

103

```
9:      {
10:         // skip the node, which already calculate the length
11:         if(length[i] > 0) continue;
12:         length[i] = consecutiveLength(num[i], hashmap, length);
13:      }
14:      int maxV = INT_MIN;
15:      for(int i =0; i< num.size(); i++)
16:      {
17:         maxV = length[i]>maxV?length[i]:maxV;
18:      }
19:      return maxV;
20: }
21: int consecutiveLength(int num,
22:      unordered_map<int, int>& hashmap,
23:      vector<int>& length)
24: {
25:      if(hashmap.find(num) == hashmap.end()) return 0;
26:      int index = hashmap[num];
27:      // skip the node, which already calculate the length
28:      if(length[index] > 0) return length[index];
29:      else
30:      {
31:         // hit each fresh node only once
32:         length[index] =
33:            consecutiveLength(num - 1, hashmap, length) + 1;
34:         return length[index];
35:      }
36: }
```

50. Longest Palindromic Substring

Given a string *S*, find the longest palindromic substring in *S*. You may assume that the maximum length of *S* is 1000, and there exists one unique longest palindromic substring.
» Solve this problem

[Thoughts]
What an interesting problem! Define P[i,j] as below:
P[i,j] = 1   if range[i,j] is a palindrome.
P[i,j] = 0   if range[i,j] is not a palindrome

Let's see an example first. Suppose S="abccb",
  S= a b c c b
Index = 0 1 2 3 4

P[0,0] =1 //each char is a palindrome
P[0,1] =S[0] == S[1]   , P[1,1] =1
P[0,2] = S[0] == S[2] && P[1,1], P[1,2] = S[1] == S[2] , P[2,2] = 1
P[0,3] = S[0] == S[3] && P[1,2], P[1,3] = S[1] == S[3] && P[2,2] ,
P[2,3] =S[2] ==S[3], P[3,3]=1
....

Base on these derivation, we can get the transition function as below:

$$P[i,j] = 1 \text{ if } i ==j$$
$$= S[i] ==S[j] \text{ if } j = i+1$$
$$= S[i] == S[j] \,\&\&\, P[i+1][j-1] \text{ if } j>i+1$$

[Code]
```
1:      string longestPalindrome(string s) {
2:          int len = s.size();
3:          int P[len][len];
4:          memset(P, 0, len*len*sizeof(int));
5:          int maxL=0, start=0, end=0;
6:          for(int i =0; i< s.size(); i++)
7:          {
8:              for(int j =0; j<i; j++)
9:              {
```

```
10:              P[j][i] = (s[j] == s[i] && (i-j<2 || P[j+1][i-1]));
11:              if(P[j][i] && maxL < (i-j+1))
12:              {
13:                  maxL = i-j+1;
14:                  start = j;
15:                  end = i;
16:              }
17:          }
18:          P[i][i] =1;
19:      }
20:      return s.substr(start, end-start +1);
21:  }
```

51. Longest Substring Without Repeating Characters

Given a string, find the length of the longest substring without repeating characters. For example, the longest substring without repeating letters for "abcabcbb" is "abc", which the length is 3.

For "bbbbb" the longest substring is "b", with the length of 1.

» Solve this problem

[Thoughts]
Scan the string from left to right. If meets repeating character, use the index of previous repeating character as the new start index of search. Keep doing this until arrives the end of string.

See below example:

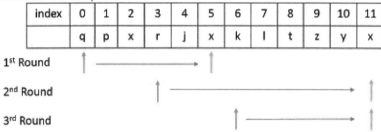

index	0	1	2	3	4	5	6	7	8	9	10	11
	q	p	x	r	j	x	k	l	t	z	y	x

1st Round

2nd Round

3rd Round

[Code]
```
1:    int lengthOfLongestSubstring(string s) {
2:        int count[26];
3:        memset(count, -1, 26*sizeof(int));
4:        int len=0, maxL = 0;
5:        for(int i =0; i< s.size(); i++,len++)
6:        {
7:            if(count[s[i]-'a']>=0)
8:            {
9:                maxL = max(len, maxL);
10:               len =0;
```

```
11:                  i = count[s[i]-'a']+1;
12:                  memset(count, -1, 26*sizeof(int));
13:              }
14:              count[s[i]-'a']=i;
15:          }
16:      return max(len, maxL);
17:  }
```

Note:
1. Line 3, since we store the index in array, so initializing the array as 0 will mistake the logic.
2. Line 16, catch the last string. for example, "abcd", if no Line 16, it will just return 0 since the Line 9 won't be triggered.

52. Longest Valid Parentheses

Given a string containing just the characters '(' and ')', find the length of the longest valid (well-formed) parentheses substring.

For "(()", the longest valid parentheses substring is "()", which has length = 2.

Another example is ")()())", where the longest valid parentheses substring is "()()", which has length = 4.

» Solve this problem

[Thoughts]
If we change this problem to "Validate whether the string is a valid parenthese", probably everyone will say "let's use stack!"

Since this problem requires to return the length of longest valid parentheses, how to solve it?

Actually, we can still use stack. Instead of pushing the character, here, we push the index of the character. So, the solution will be

```
If the char is '(', push the index of
current '('

If the char is ')', pop the latest '(' index
from stack, calculate the length, and update
the max track if needed.
```

[Code]

```
1:  int longestValidParentheses(string s) {
2:      const char* str = s.c_str();
3:      int nMax=0;
4:      const char *p = str;
5:      vector<const char*> sta;
6:      while(*p !='\0')
7:      {
```

```
8:        if(*p == '(')
9:        {
10:           sta.push_back(p);
11:        }
12:        else
13:        {
14:           if(!sta.empty() && *sta.back()=='(')
15:           {
16:              sta.pop_back();
17:              nMax = max(nMax,
18:                      p- (sta.empty()?str-1:sta.back()) );
19:           }
20:           else
21:           {
22:              sta.push_back(p);
23:           }
24:        }
25:        p++;
26:     }
27:     return nMax;
28: }
```

53. LRU Cache

Design and implement a data structure for Least Recently Used
(LRU) cache. It should support the following
operations: `get` and `set`.

`get(key)` - Get the value (will always be positive) of the key if
the key exists in the cache, otherwise return -1.
`set(key, value)` - Set or insert the value if the key is not
already present. When the cache reached its capacity, it should
invalidate the least recently used item before inserting a new
item.

[Thoughts]
For the cache, we expect to index the target in O(1). It's pretty
straightforward to use hashmap for storing the mapping between
key and value. But since this problem also requires LRU policy
as a build-in feature of the cache, the challenge here changes to
how to retire the cache entry and restructure the order in O(1).

Let's say, we store the cache entry in a list.Suppose we can
gurantee the list is sorted by timestamp. So, the head of the list
is the freshest cache entry, and the tail of the list is the oldest
cache entry. We have two scenarios:

1. If user visits a cache entry C_k, we need move C_k to the
   head of the list since it becomes the freshest entry now.
2. If user inserts a cache entry C_{new}, put C_{new} as the new
   head of the list and delete the tail if the list is already full
   of capacity.

As the implementation, we need two data structures:
1. List. Store the cache entry by the order of timestamp.
2. Hashmap. Store the key and the **INDEX** of the cache
   entry in the list

[Code]

```
1: class LRUCache{
2: public:
```

111

```
3:    struct CacheEntry
4:    {
5:    public:
6:        int key;
7:        int value;
8:        CacheEntry(int k, int v) :key(k), value(v) {}
9:    };
10:    LRUCache(int capacity) {
11:        m_capacity = capacity;
12:    }
13:    int get(int key) {
14:        if (m_map.find(key) == m_map.end())
15:            return -1;
16:        MoveToHead(key);
17:        return m_map[key]->value;
18:    }
19:    void set(int key, int value) {
20:        if (m_map.find(key) == m_map.end())
21:        {
22:            CacheEntry newItem(key, value);
23:            if (m_LRU_cache.size() >= m_capacity)
24:            {
25:                //remove from tail
26:                m_map.erase(m_LRU_cache.back().key);
27:                m_LRU_cache.pop_back();
28:            }
29:            // insert in head.
30:            m_LRU_cache.push_front(newItem);
31:            m_map[key] = m_LRU_cache.begin();
32:            return;
33:        }
34:        m_map[key]->value = value;
35:        MoveToHead(key);
36:    }
37: private:
```

```
38:     unordered_map<int, list<CacheEntry>::iterator> m_map;
39:     list<CacheEntry> m_LRU_cache;
40:     int m_capacity;
41:     void MoveToHead(int key)
42:     {
43:         //Move key from current location to head
44:         auto updateEntry = *m_map[key];
45:         m_LRU_cache.erase(m_map[key]);
46:         m_LRU_cache.push_front(updateEntry);
47:         m_map[key] = m_LRU_cache.begin();
48:     }
49: };
```

54.   Maximum Depth of Binary Tree

Given a binary tree, find its maximum depth.
The maximum depth is the number of nodes along the longest path from the root node down to the farthest leaf node.
» Solve this problem

[Thoughts]
Define Max[K] as the maximal depth of node K(no matter where this K is in the tree). We can derive the transition function as
        Max [K] = max (Max[K->left] , Max[K->right]) + 1
And, implement it as below.

[Code]
```
1:   int maxDepth(TreeNode *root) {
2:     // Start typing your C/C++ solution below
3:     // DO NOT write int main() function
4:     if(root == NULL)
5:        return 0;
6:     int lmax = maxDepth(root->left);
7:     int rmax = maxDepth(root->right);
8:     return max(lmax, rmax)+1;
9:   }
```

Another solution is to traverse the tree in level order and count the level. You can refer to the problem " Binary Tree Level Order Traversal" in the later chapter.

55. Max Points on a Line

Given *n* points on a 2D plane, find the maximum number of points that lie on the same straight line.

[Thoughts]
For any straight line, it could be defined as

```
y = ax + b
```

Assume, there are point A(x1,y1) and B(x2,y2). If they are in the same line, we can get following equations:

y1 = kx1 +b   [1]
y2 = kx2 +b   [2]

[2] – [1] => k = (y2-y1)/(x2-x1). K is the slop of line AB. If there is a another point C, and the slop of line CB is also k. Based on transitivity, we know A, B, C are in the same line.\

So, the solution is, iterate the point one by one. For any iterated point (xk,yk), calculate the slop between (xk, yk) and every left points. All the points with same slop are in the same line. Count the points and return the max count in the end.

[Code]
Two cases need special logic:
1. Vertical line. The slop is ∞
2. Duplicate points.

```
1: int maxPoints(vector<Point> &points) {
2:    unordered_map<float, int> statistic;
3:    int maxNum = 0;
4:    for (int i = 0; i< points.size(); i++)
5:    {
6:        statistic.clear();
7:        statistic[INT_MIN] = 0; // for processing duplicate point
8:        int duplicate = 1;
9:        for (int j = 0; j<points.size(); j++)
10:       {
11:           if (j == i) continue;
12:           if (points[j].x == points[i].x &&
                      points[j].y == points[i].y) // count duplicate
13:           {
```

```
14:                duplicate++;
15:                continue;
16:            }
17:            float key = (points[j].x - points[i].x) == 0 ?
18:                INT_MAX :  (float) (points[j].y - points[i].y) /
(points[j].x - points[i].x);
19:                statistic[key]++;
20:        }
21:        for (auto& it = statistic.begin(); it != statistic.end(); ++it)
22:        {
23:            if (it->second + duplicate >maxNum)
24:            {
25:                maxNum = it->second + duplicate;
26:            }
27:        }
28:    }
29:    return maxNum;
30: }
```

56. Maximum Subarray

Find the contiguous subarray within an array (containing at least one number) which has the largest sum.
For example, given the array $[-2,1,-3,4,-1,2,1,-5,4]$,
the contiguous subarray $[4,-1,2,1]$ has the largest sum = 6.
More practice:
If you have figured out the O(n) solution, try coding another solution using the divide and conquer approach, which is more subtle.
» Solve this problem

[Thoughts]
Use one dimensional dynamic programming to achieve a O(n) complexity.

Assume there is a K existing in A(0, i), which makes A[k, i] generating the largest sum Max[i].

So, for Max[i+1], it's easy to know get following transition function:

```
Max[i+1] = Max[i] + A[i+1],   if (Max[i] +
A[i+1] >0)
         = 0, if(Max[i]+A[i+1] <0), the
reason here is, A[i+1] must be a negative
number, which has no value to keep.
```

Scan the array from left to right and easy to find the largest sum.

[Code]
```
1: int maxSubArray(int A[], int n) {
2:     int sum = 0;
3:     int max = INT_MIN;
4:     for(int i =0; i < n ; i ++)
5:     {
6:         sum +=A[i];
7:         if(sum>max)
```

```
8:              max = sum;
9:          if(sum < 0)
10:             sum = 0;
11:     }
12:     return max;
13: }
```

But this problem requires Divide & Conquer. It hints us to use binary search.

Suppose there exits a range [i,j], which generates the largest sum in A[left, right]. If use the middle value(mid = (left + right)/2) to split the range, there are 3 conditions:

> (1) subarray A[i,..j] is entirely in A[low,mid-1]
> (2) subarray A[i,..j] is entirely in A[mid+1,high]
> (3) subarray A[i,..j] is across mid

For Condition #1 and #2, just continue to do the recursion. But for Condition #3, it's a little tricky. Need to search bi-direction. Search A[left, Mid] to find the max range [i..mid], search A[mid+1, right] for A[mid+1..j], and merge A[i.. mid] and A[mide+1.. j] together as the solution of Condition #3.

Implement as below :

```
1:  int maxSubArray(int A[], int n) {
2:      int maxV = INT_MIN;
3:      return maxArray(A, 0, n-1, maxV);
4:  }
5:  int maxArray(int A[], int left, int right, int& maxV)
6:  {
7:      if(left>right)
8:          return INT_MIN;
9:      int mid = (left+right)/2;
10:     int lmax = maxArray(A, left, mid -1, maxV);
11:     int rmax = maxArray(A, mid + 1, right, maxV);
12:     maxV = max(maxV, lmax);
```

```
13:     maxV = max(maxV, rmax);
14:     int sum = 0, mlmax = 0;
15:     for(int i= mid -1; i>=left; i--)
16:     {
17:        sum += A[i];
18:        if(sum > mlmax)
19:           mlmax = sum;
20:     }
21:     sum = 0; int mrmax = 0;
22:     for(int i = mid +1; i<=right; i++)
23:     {
24:        sum += A[i];
25:        if(sum > mrmax)
26:           mrmax = sum;
27:     }
28:     maxV = max(maxV, mlmax + mrmax + A[mid]);
29:     return maxV;
30: }
31:
```

57. Median of Two Sorted Arrays

There are two sorted arrays A and B of size m and n respectively. Find the median of the two sorted arrays. The overall run time complexity should be O(log (m+n)).
» Solve this problem

[Thoughts]
The solution to O(n) is intuitive: directly merge two arrays, then seek the median.

However, to O(log(m+n)), obviously binary-search is the solution. This is equivalent to the variation of "Kth element in 2 sorted array". If (m+n) is odd, then find "(m+n)/2+1 th element in 2 sorted array". If (m+n) is even, find (m+n)/2 th and (m+n)/2+1 th, then average them.

With regard to "Kth element in 2 sorted array" , the two arrays can be divided into four parts as the following diagram by the two medians A[m/2] and B[n/2]. Abandoning which part depends on two conditions:

```
1,  (m/2 + n/2)?k;
2,  A[m/2] ? B[n/2];
```

$$a_0, a_1, a_2, \ldots a_{m/2}, a_{m/2+1}, \ldots a_{m-2}, a_{m-1}$$

| Section 1 | Section 2 |

$$b_0, b_1, b_2, \ldots b_{n/2}, b_{n/2+1}, \ldots b_{n-2}, b_{n-1}$$

| Section 3 | Section 4 |

1. $(m/2+n/2+1)$? k
2. $a_{m/2}$? $b_{n/2}$

If (m/2 + n/2) > k, that means the current median is higher, the correct median is in either Section 1 or Section 3. If A[m/2] >

B[n/2], it means the median is absolutely not in Section 2, so this section will be abandon for the new search. Likewise, the rest three circumstances can be deduced as the following formulas:

```
If (m/2+n/2+1) > k && a_m/2 > b_n/2 ,
drop Section 2
If (m/2+n/2+1) > k && a_m/2 < b_n/2 ,
drop Section 4
If (m/2+n/2+1) < k && a_m/2 > b_n/2
, drop Section 3
If (m/2+n/2+1) < k &&
a_m/2 < b_n/2 , drop Section 1
```

To be simple, it is to abandon the right section to the biggest median or the left section to the smallest median.

[Code]
Note line 12~14. The terminal condition of recursion when n==0, m ==0, and k==1.

```
1:  double findMedianSortedArrays(int A[], int m, int B[], int n) {
2:      if((n+m)%2 ==0)
3:      {
4:          return (GetMedian(A,m,B,n, (m+n)/2)
5:              + GetMedian(A,m,B,n, (m+n)/2+1))/2.0;
6:      }
7:      else
8:          return GetMedian(A,m,B,n, (m+n)/2+1);
9:  }
10:
11: int GetMedian(int a[], int n, int b[], int m, int k)
12: {
13:     assert(a && b);
14:     if (n <= 0) return b[k-1];
15:     if (m <= 0) return a[k-1];
16:     if (k <= 1) return min(a[0], b[0]);
17:     if (b[m/2] >= a[n/2])
18:     {
```

121

```
19:        if ((n/2 + 1 + m/2) >= k)
20:            return GetMedian(a, n, b, m/2, k);
21:        else
22:            return GetMedian(
23:                a + n/2 + 1, n - (n/2 + 1), b, m, k - (n/2 + 1));
24:    }
25:    else
26:    {
27:        if ((m/2 + 1 + n/2) >= k)
28:            return GetMedian( a, n/2,b, m, k);
29:        else
30:            return GetMedian(
31:                a, n, b + m/2 + 1, m - (m/2 + 1),k - (m/2 + 1));
32:    }
33: }
34:
```

58. Merge Intervals

Given a collection of intervals, merge all overlapping intervals.

For example,

Given `[1,3]`,`[2,6]`,`[8,10]`,`[15,18]`,

return `[1,6]`,`[8,10]`,`[15,18]`.
» Solve this problem

[Thoughts]
Reuse the solution code from prior "Insert Intervals". Create a new empty collection. Then, pick the interval from old collection one by one and insert it into new collection. That's it,

[Code]
```
1:  vector<Interval> merge(vector<Interval> &intervals) {
2:      vector<Interval> result;
3:      for(int i =0; i< intervals.size(); i++)
4:      {
5:          insert(result, intervals[i]);
6:      }
7:      return result;
8:  }
9:  void insert(vector<Interval> &intervals, Interval newInterval) {
10:     vector<Interval>::iterator it = intervals.begin();
11:     while(it!= intervals.end())
12:     {
13:         if(newInterval.end<it->start)
14:         {
15:             intervals.insert(it, newInterval);
16:             return;
17:         }
18:         else if(newInterval.start > it->end)
19:         {
20:             it++;
21:             continue;
22:         }
```

```
23:        else
24:        {
25:            newInterval.start = min(newInterval.start, it->start);
26:            newInterval.end = max(newInterval.end, it->end);
27:            it =intervals.erase(it);
28:        }
29:    }
30:    intervals.insert(intervals.end(), newInterval);
31: }
```

59. Merge k Sorted Lists

Merge *k* sorted linked lists and return it as one sorted list.
Analyze and describe its complexity.
» Solve this problem

[Thoughts]
Merge sort. Only need to pay attention of pointer operation.

[Code]
```
1:   ListNode *mergeKLists(vector<ListNode *> &lists) {
2:     if(lists.size() == 0) return NULL;
3:     ListNode *p = lists[0];
4:     for(int i =1; i< lists.size(); i++)
5:     {
6:       p = merge2Lists(p, lists[i]);
7:     }
8:     return p;
9:   }
10:    ListNode * merge2Lists(ListNode *head1, ListNode *head2)
11:    {
12:      ListNode *head = new ListNode(INT_MIN);
13:      ListNode *p = head;
14:      while(head1!=NULL && head2!=NULL)
15:      {
16:        if(head1->val < head2->val)
17:        {
18:          p->next = head1;
19:          head1 = head1->next;
20:        }
21:        else
22:        {
23:          p->next = head2;
24:          head2 = head2->next;
25:        }
26:        p = p->next;
```

```
27:    }
28:    if(head1 !=NULL)
29:    {
30:      p->next = head1;
31:    }
32:    if(head2 != NULL)
33:    {
34:      p->next = head2;
35:    }
36:    p = head;
37:    head = head->next;
38:    delete p;
39:    return head;
40:  }
```

60. Merge Sorted Array

Given two sorted integer arrays A and B, merge B into A as one sorted array.

Note:

You may assume that A has enough space to hold additional elements from B. The number of elements initialized in A and B are *m* and *n* respectively.

» Solve this problem

[Thoughts]

Did you play a game to fill the blank with some characters in order. This problem actually uses the same idea.

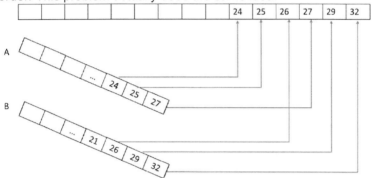

But unfortunately, we don't have extra array to fill. As problem mentioned, A has lots of blank space inside. So use A as the extrac space. But need to fill the blank from back to front, or the content of array A will be polluted.

[Code]

```
1:   void merge(int A[], int m, int B[], int n) {
2:      int k = m+n-1;
3:      int i = m-1, j =n-1;
4:      for(; i>=0 && j>=0; k--)
5:      {
6:         if(A[i] >= B[j])
7:         {
8:            A[k] = A[i];
9:            i--;
```

127

```
10:      }
11:      else
12:      {
13:        A[k] = B[j];
14:        j--;
15:      }
16:    }
17:    while(j >=0)
18:    {
19:      A[k] = B[j];
20:      k--; j--;
21:    }
22:  }
```

61. Merge Two Sorted Lists

Merge two sorted linked lists and return it as a new list. The new list should be made by splicing together the nodes of the first two lists.
» Solve this problem

[Thoughts]
This is just a implementation problem. Take care of the pointer operation.

[Code]

```
1:  ListNode *mergeTwoLists(ListNode *l1, ListNode *l2) {
2:      ListNode* head = new ListNode(-1);
3:      ListNode* p = head;
4:      while(l1!=NULL || l2!= NULL)
5:      {
6:          int val1 = l1==NULL?INT_MAX:l1->val;
7:          int val2 = l2==NULL? INT_MAX:l2->val;
8:          if(val1<=val2)
9:          {
10:             p->next = l1;
11:             l1=l1->next;
12:         }
13:         else
14:         {
15:             p->next = l2;
16:             l2 = l2->next;
17:         }
18:         p= p->next;
19:     }
20:     p = head->next;
21:     delete head;
22:     return p;
23: }
```

62. Minimum Depth of Binary Tree

Given a binary tree, find its minimum depth.

The minimum depth is the number of nodes along the shortest path from the root node down to the nearest leaf node.

» Solve this problem

[Thoughts]
Recursion is the best friend of tree-related problems. Same here. If we define Min[K] as the minimal depth of node K(no matter where this K is in the tree). We can derive the transition function as

Min[K] = min (Min[K->left] , Min[K->right]) + 1

And, implement it as below.

[Code]
```
1:   int minDepth(TreeNode *root) {
2:     // Start typing your C/C++ solution below
3:     // DO NOT write int main() function
4:     if(root == NULL)
5:       return 0;
6:     int lmin = minDepth(root->left);
7:     int rmin = minDepth(root->right);
8:     if(lmin ==0 && rmin ==0)
9:       return 1;
10:    if(lmin ==0)
11:    {
12:      lmin = INT_MAX;
13:    }
14:    if(rmin ==0)
15:    {
16:      rmin = INT_MAX;
17:    }
18:    return min(lmin, rmin) +1;
19:  }
```

63. Minimum Path Sum

Given a *m* x *n* grid filled with non-negative numbers, find a path
from top left to bottom right which *minimizes* the sum of all
numbers along its path.
Note: You can only move either down or right at any point in
time.
» Solve this problem

[Thoughts]
Two-dimension dynamic programming. Let's use A[row][col] to
represent the m x n grid. Define Min[i][j] as the minimal sum of
cell (i,j).

Since problem already requires that the path from top left to
bottom right, so for cell (i,j), the path can only come from either
(i-1,j) or (i,j-1)

It's easy to get the transition function:

```
Min[i][j] =   min ( Min[i-1][j],   Min[i][j-1]
) + A[i][j]   if i>0 && j>0
       or =   A[0][j]   if i==0
       or =   A[i][0]   if j==0
```

[Code]
```
1:  int minPathSum(vector<vector<int> > &grid) {
2:    // Start typing your C/C++ solution below
3:    // DO NOT write int main() function
```

131

```
4:    if(grid.size() ==0) return 0;
5:    int row = grid.size();
6:    int col = grid[0].size();
7:    int Min[row][col];
8:    Min[0][0] =grid[0][0];
9:    for(int i =1; i < row; i ++)
10:   {
11:     Min[i][0] =Min[i-1][0] + grid[i][0];
12:   }
13:   for(int i =1; i< col; i++)
14:   {
15:     Min[0][i] = Min[0][i-1] + grid[0][i];
16:   }
17:   for(int i =1; i< row; i++)
18:   {
19:     for(int j =1; j< col; j++)
20:     {
21:       Min[i][j] = min(Min[i-1][j], Min[i][j-1]) + grid[i][j];
22:     }
23:   }
24:   return Min[row-1][col-1];
25: }
```

Previous code uses a two- dimension array to track and compute
Min. But in real implementation, use a one- dimension iterative
array is enough. Below code is more beautiful.

```
1:   int minPathSum(vector<vector<int> > &grid) {
2:     int row = grid.size();
3:     if(row == 0) return 0;
4:     int col = grid[0].size();
5:     if(col == 0) return 0;
6:     vector<int> steps(col, INT_MAX);
7:     steps[0] =0;
8:     for(int i =0; i< row; i++)
```

```
9:    {
10:       steps[0] = steps[0] + grid[i][0];
11:       for(int j=1; j<col; j++)
12:       {
13:           steps[j]=min(steps[j], steps[j-1]) + grid[i][j];
14:       }
15:    }
16:    return steps[col-1];
17: }
```

64. Minimum Window Substring

Given a string S and a string T, find the minimum window in S which will contain all the characters in T in complexity O(n).
For example,
S = "ADOBECODEBANC"
T = "ABC"
Minimum window is "BANC".
Note:
If there is no such window in S that covers all characters in T, return the emtpy string "".
If there are multiple such windows, you are guaranteed that there will always be only one unique minimum window in S.
» Solve this problem

[Thoughts]
Use two pointers to maintain a window dynamically. The tail pointer keep moving forward. If the window contains all the characters in T, try to shrink the window by moving head pointer forward. When the window can't be shrinked, track the window size if it is the minimal one.

[Code]
```
1:    string minWindow(string S, string T) {
2:     // Start typing your C/C++ solution below
3:     // DO NOT write int main() function
4:       if(S.size() == 0) return "";
5:        if(S.size() < T.size()) return "";
6:        int appearCount[256];
7:        int expectCount[256];
8:        memset(appearCount, 0, 256*sizeof(appearCount[0]));
9:        memset(expectCount, 0, 256*sizeof(appearCount[0]));
10:       for(int i =0; i < T.size(); i++)
11:       {
12:           expectCount[T[i]]++;
13:       }
14:       int minV = INT_MAX, min_start = 0;
```

```
15:        int wid_start=0;
16:        int appeared = 0;
17:        for(int wid_end = 0; wid_end< S.size(); wid_end++)
18:        {
19:            if(expectCount[S[wid_end]] > 0)//his char is a part
of T
20:            {
21:                appearCount[S[wid_end]]++;
22:                if(appearCount[S[wid_end]] <=
expectCount[S[wid_end]])
23:                    appeared ++;
24:            }
25:            if(appeared == T.size())
26:            {
27:                while(appearCount[S[wid_start]] >
expectCount[S[wid_start]]
28:                    || expectCount[S[wid_start]] == 0)
29:                {
30:                    appearCount[S[wid_start]]--;
31:                    wid_start ++;
32:                }
33:                if(minV > (wid_end - wid_start +1))
34:                {
35:                    minV = wid_end - wid_start +1;
36:                    min_start = wid_start;
37:                }
38:            }
39:        }
40:    if(minV == INT_MAX) return "";
41:        return S.substr(min_start, minV);
42: }
```

65. Multiply Strings

Given two numbers represented as strings, return multiplication of the numbers as a string.
Note: The numbers can be arbitrarily large and are non-negative.
» Solve this problem

[Thoughts]
Big integer multiplication. Just implementation. Multiply the digit one by one. Pay more attention on the carry bit and also Zero. For example, Line 25~31, skip the redundant zero. "9133", "0", the multiply result will be "000000", but user only need one zero --"0".

[Code]
```
1:   string multiply(string num1, string num2) {
2:      // Start typing your C/C++ solution below
3:      // DO NOT write int main() function
4:      if(num1.size() ==0 || num2.size() ==0) return 0;
5:      string res(num1.size()+num2.size()+1, '0');
6:      std::reverse(num1.begin(), num1.end());
7:      std::reverse(num2.begin(), num2.end());
8:      for(int i =0; i < num1.size(); i++)
9:      {
10:        int dig1 = num1[i] -'0';
11:        int carry = 0;
12:        for(int j = 0; j< num2.size(); j++)
13:        {
14:          int dig2 = num2[j] - '0';
15:          int exist = res[i+j] -'0';
16:          res[i+j] = (dig1*dig2+carry+ exist) % 10 +'0';
17:          carry = (dig1*dig2+carry+exist)/10;
18:        }
19:        if(carry >0)
20:        {
21:          res[i+num2.size()] = carry + '0';
```

```
22:      }
23:    }
24:    std::reverse(res.begin(), res.end());
25:    int start =0;
26:    while(res[start] =='0' && start < res.size())
27:    {
28:      start++;
29:    }
30:    if(start == res.size()) return "0";
31:    return res.substr(start, res.size()-start);
32:  }
```

66. Next Permutation

Implement next permutation, which rearranges numbers into the lexicographically next greater permutation of numbers.

If such arrangement is not possible, it must rearrange it as the lowest possible order (ie, sorted in ascending order).

The replacement must be in-place, do not allocate extra memory.

Here are some examples. Inputs are in the left-hand column and its corresponding outputs are in the right-hand column.

$1,2,3 \rightarrow 1,3,2$
$3,2,1 \rightarrow 1,2,3$
$1,1,5 \rightarrow 1,5,1$

» Solve this problem

[Thoughts]

More like a math problem. Below example demonstrates how to get the next permutation of 687432.

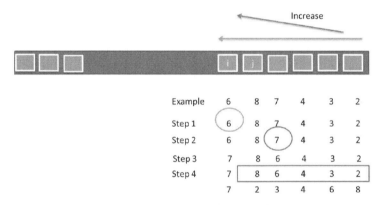

1. From right to left, find the first digit (PartitionNumber)which violate the increase trend, in this example, 6 will be selected since 8,7,4,3,2 already in a increase trend.
2. From right to left, find the first digit which large than PartitionNumber, call it changeNumber. Here the 7 will be selected.
3. Swap the PartitionNumber and ChangeNumber.
4. Reverse all the digit on the right of partition index.

[Code]

```
1:    void nextPermutation(vector<int> &num) {
2:        assert(num.size() >0);
3:        int vioIndex = num.size() -1;
4:        while(vioIndex >0)
5:        {
6:            if(num[vioIndex-1] < num[vioIndex])
7:                break;
8:            vioIndex --;
9:        }
10:       if(vioIndex >0)
11:       {
12:           vioIndex--;
13:           int rightIndex = num.size()-1;
14:           while(rightIndex >=0 && num[rightIndex] <=
num[vioIndex])
15:           {
16:               rightIndex --;
17:           }
18:           int swap = num[vioIndex];
10:           num[vioIndex] = num[rightIndex];
20:           num[rightIndex] = swap;
21:           vioIndex++;
22:       }
23:       int end= num.size()-1;
24:       while(end > vioIndex)
25:       {
26:           int swap = num[vioIndex];
27:           num[vioIndex] = num[end];
28:           num[end] = swap;
29:           end--;
30:           vioIndex++;
31:       }
32:   }
```

67. Palindrome Number

Determine whether an integer is a palindrome. Do this without extra space.
Some hints:
Could negative integers be palindromes? (ie, -1)
If you are thinking of converting the integer to string, note the restriction of using extra space. You could also try reversing an integer. However, if you have solved the problem "Reverse Integer", you know that the reversed integer might overflow. How would you handle such case? There is a more generic way of solving this problem.
» Solve this problem

[Thoughts]
Split the first digit and the last digit out , and compare them. If they are equal, continue to split the second one and the last but one, etc. until no digit left or find non-equal digits.

[Code]
```
1:      bool isPalindrome(int x) {
2:          if(x<0) return false;
3:          int div = 1;
4:          while(x/div >=10)
5:              div*=10;
6:          while(x>0)
7:          {
8:              int l = x/div;
9:              int r = x%10;
10:             if(l!=r) return false;
11:             x=x%div/10;
12:             div/=100;
13:         }
14:         return true;
15:     }
```

68. Palindrome Partitioning

Given a string *s*, partition *s* such that every substring of the partition is a palindrome.

Return all possible palindrome partitioning of *s*.

For example, given *s* = `"aab"`,

Return

```
[
    ["aa","b"],
    ["a","a","b"]
]
```

» Solve this problem

[Thoughts]
In general, if the problem asks to output all the possible solutions. It's better to use DFS to solve for simple coding. But if the problem asks for the best solution or the count of all the possible solutions, it implys that you need to use DP.

[Code]

```
1:  vector<vector<string>> partition(string s) {
2:      vector<vector<string>> result;
3:      vector<string> output;
4:      DFS(s, 0, output, result);
5:      return result;
6:  }
7:  void DFS(string &s, int start, vector<string>& output,
8:           vector<vector<string>> &result)
9:  {
10:     if(start == s.size())
11:     {
12:         result.push_back(output);
```

```
13:         return;
14:     }
15:     for(int i = start; i< s.size(); i++)
16:     {
17:         if(isPalindrome(s, start, i))
18:         {
19:             output.push_back(s.substr(start, i-start+1));
20:             DFS(s, i+1, output, result);
21:             output.pop_back();
22:         }
23:     }
24: }
25: bool isPalindrome(string &s, int start, int end)
26: {
27:     while(start< end)
28:     {
29:         if(s[start] != s[end])
30:             return false;
31:         start++; end--;
32:     }
33:     return true;
34: }
```

69. Palindrome Partitioning II

Given a string s, partition s such that every substring of the partition is a palindrome.

Return the minimum cuts needed for a palindrome partitioning of s.

For example, given s = `"aab"`,

Return `1` since the palindrome partitioning `["aa","b"]` could be produced using 1 cut.

» Solve this problem

[Thoughts]
Since this problem looks for the minimum cuts, it is pretty normal to use DP to solve this problem.

Let's define the DP function first.

```
D[i,n] = the minimum cus of range [i,n] (n
is the length of input string S).
```

Look at below example.

a b a b b b a b b a b a
      i   n

How to calculate the D[i,n]? we can iterate the every elemnts between [i, n] and set it as j.

a b a b b b a b b a b a
      i   j j+1   n

Here, we can see

```
D[i, n] = min(D[i, j] + D[j+1,n])    i<=j <n.
```

Looks this is a two-dimensional dynamic programming, which is a little heavy to write the code. In the formula, the extra variable is n. Could we get rid of it? Yes, actually we don't need n. In the iteration, we only calculate the D[i,n] if S[i,j] is a palindrome.

So, let's introduce another function.

143

```
P[i][j]  = true, if S[i,j] is a palindrome
         = false, if not.
```

So the D function could be changed to

```
D[i] = the minimum cus of range [i,n]  (n is the
length of input string S).

D[i] = min(1+D[j+1] )     i<=j <n  if P[i][j]
= true
```

[Code]

```
1:  int minCut(string s) {
2:      int len = s.size();
3:      int D[len+1];
4:      bool P[len][len];
5:      //the worst case is cutting by each char
6:      for(int i = 0; i <= len; i++)
7:          D[i] = len-i;
8:      for(int i = 0; i < len; i++)
9:          for(int j = 0; j < len; j++)
10:             P[i][j] = false;
11:     for(int i = len-1; i >= 0; i--){
12:         for(int j = i; j < len; j++){
13:             if(s[i] == s[j] && (j-i<2 || P[i+1][j-1])){
14:                 P[i][j] = true;
15:                 D[i] = min(D[i],D[j+1]+1);
16:             }
17:         }
18:     }
19:     return D[0]-1;
20: }
```

70. Partition List

Given a linked list and a value *x*, partition it such that all nodes less than *x* come before nodes greater than or equal to *x*.
You should preserve the original relative order of the nodes in each of the two partitions.
For example,
Given 1->4->3->2->5->2 and *x* = 3,
return 1->2->2->4->3->5.
» Solve this problem

[Thoughts]
Scan from left to right. Find the first node K which is larger than X. And for any node which is less than X, insert it on the left of K. And here, introduce a SafeGuard node(fake head) to avoid processing head node.

[Code]
```
1:  ListNode *partition(ListNode *head, int x) {
2:      ListNode* p = new ListNode(x-1);
3:      p->next = head;
4:      head = p;
5:      ListNode* pre;
6:      while(p!=NULL && p->val < x)
7:      {
8:          pre = p;
9:          p = p->next;
10:     }
11:     if(p!=NULL)
12:     {
13:         //Track the insert position.
14:         ListNode* cur = pre;
15:         while(p!=NULL)
16:         {
17:             if(p->val <x)
18:             {
19:                 ListNode* temp = cur->next;
```

```
20:            pre->next = p->next;
21:            cur->next = p;
22:            cur = p;
23:            p->next = temp;
24:            p = pre;
25:        }
26:        pre=p;
27:        p= p->next;
28:     }
29:  }
30:  ListNode* temp = head;
31:  head = head->next;
32:  delete temp;
33:  return head;
34: }
35:
```

71. Pascal's Triangle II

Given an index k, return the kth row of the Pascal's triangle.
For example, given $k = 3$,
Return $[1,3,3,1]$.

```
[
     [1],
    [1,1],
   [1,2,1],
  [1,3,3,1],
 [1,4,6,4,1]
]
```

Note:
Could you optimize your algorithm to use only $O(k)$ extra space?
» Solve this problem

[Thoughts]
Dynamic programming.
Justify the sample by left as below:

```
[
 [1],
 [1,1],
 [1,2,1],
 [1,3,3,1],
 [1,4,6,4,1]
]
```

Define T[i][j] as the element in the left-justified triangle. And we can get the transition function as,

```
T[i][j] = T[i-1][j] + T[i-1][j-1] if i>0 && j>0
     Or
        =   1   if i=0
     Or
        =  T[i-1][j]   if j=0
```

In the real implementation, we can use 1D array to calculate iteratively. For each level, compute from right to left. Think why?

147

[Code]

```
1:  vector<int> getRow(int rowIndex) {
2:      vector<int> result;
3:      result.resize(rowIndex+2);
4:      for(int i =0; i< rowIndex+2; i++)
5:      result[i] = 0;
6:      result[1]=1;
7:      for(int i =0; i< rowIndex; i++)
8:      {
9:          //from right to left. avoid duplicate add
10:         for(int j =rowIndex+1; j>0; j--)
11:         {
12:             result[j] = result[j-1] + result[j];
13:         }
14:     }
15:     result.erase(result.begin());
16:     return result;
17: }
18:
```

72. Path Sum

Given a binary tree and a sum, determine if the tree has a root-to-leaf path such that adding up all the values along the path equals the given sum.
For example:
Given the below binary tree and `sum = 22`,

```
            5
           / \
          4   8
         /   / \
        11  13  4
       /  \      \
      7    2      1
```

return true, as there exist a root-to-leaf path `5->4->11->2` which sum is 22.
» Solve this problem

[Thoughts]
Traversal of a binary tree. Add up the node values while traversing, when approach any leaf node, compare the sum with expect value, if they equal, then return, or give up this path.

[Code]
```
1:    bool hasPathSum(TreeNode *root, int sum) {
2:        return hasPathSum(root, 0, sum);
3:    }
4:    bool hasPathSum(TreeNode *root, int sum, int target) {
5:        if(root == NULL) return false;
6:        sum += root->val;
7:        if(root->left == NULL && root->right == NULL) //leaf
8:        {
9:            if(sum == target)
10:               return true;
11:           else
```

```
12:            return false;
13:        }
14:    return hasPathSum(root->left, sum, target)
15:        || hasPathSum(root->right, sum, target);
16:    }
```

73. Path Sum II

Given a binary tree and a sum, find all root-to-leaf paths where each path's sum equals the given sum.
For example:
Given the below binary tree and `sum = 22`,

```
                5
               / \
              4   8
             /   / \
            11  13  4
           / \    / \
          7   2  5   1
```

return

```
[
    [5,4,11,2],
    [5,8,4,5]
]
```

» Solve this problem

[Thoughts]
Similar as previous one. But add extra logic to record all the solution paths as highlight code.

[Code]
```
1:  vector<vector<int> > pathSum(TreeNode *root, int sum) {
2:      vector<vector<int> > collect;
3:      vector<int> solution;
4:      if(root!=NULL)
5:          GetPath(root, sum, 0, solution, collect);
6:      return collect;
7:  }
8:  void GetPath(TreeNode* node, int sum, int cal,
9:      vector<int>& solution, vector<vector<int> >& collect)
```

```
10:  {
11:      solution.push_back(node->val);
12:      cal += node->val;
13:      if(cal == sum
14:              && node->left == NULL
15:              && node->right == NULL)
16:      {
17:          collect.push_back(solution);
18:      }
19:      else
20:      {
21:          if(node->left != NULL)
22:          {
23:              GetPath(node->left, sum, cal, solution, collect);
24:          }
25:          if(node->right != NULL)
26:          {
27:              GetPath(node->right, sum, cal, solution, collect);
28:          }
29:      }
30:      solution.pop_back();
31:      return;
32: }
33:
```

74. Permutations

Given a collection of numbers, return all possible permutations.
For example,
[1,2,3] have the following permutations:
[1,2,3], [1,3,2], [2,1,3], [2,3,1], [3,1,2], and [3,2,1].

» Solve this problem

[Thoughts]
A classic recursion problem. And need a array to track the visit status of each number for avoiding duplicated visit.

[Code]
```
1:  vector<vector<int> > permute(vector<int> &num) {
2:      vector<vector<int> > coll;
3:      vector<int> solution;
4:      if(num.size() ==0) return coll;
5:      vector<int> visited(num.size(), 0);
6:      GeneratePermute(num, 0, visited, solution, coll);
7:      return coll;
8:  }
9:
10: void GeneratePermute(vector<int> & num, int step,
11:     vector<int>& visited,
12:     vector<int>& solution,
13:     vector<vector<int> >& coll)
14: {
15:     if(step == num.size())
16:     {
17:         coll.push_back(solution);
18:         return;
19:     }
20:     for(int i =0; i< num.size(); i++)
21:     {
22:         // if this number already used, skip it
23:         if(visited[i] == 0)
```

```
24:          {
25:              visited[i] = 1;
26:              solution.push_back(num[i]);
27:              GeneratePermute(
28:                  num, step+1, visited, solution, coll);
29:              solution.pop_back();
30:              visited[i] =0;
31:          }
32:      }
33: }
34:
```

75. Permutations II

Given a collection of numbers that might contain duplicates,
return all possible unique permutations.
For example,
[1,1,2] have the following unique permutations:
[1,1,2], [1,2,1], and [2,1,1].
» Solve this problem

[Thoughts]
Same thoughts as previous problem. But this time, need extro
logic to de-duplicate. So sort the array first, and when DFS the
solution, skip unnecessary processing if the previous number is
same as current one. Comparing with previous problem
'Permutation', the highlight part are the only changes.

[Code]
```
1:  vector<vector<int> > permuteUnique(vector<int> &num) {
2:      vector<vector<int> > coll;
3:      vector<int> solution;
4:      if(num.size() ==0) return coll;
5:      vector<int> visited(num.size(), 0);
6:      sort(num.begin(), num.end());
7:      GeneratePermute(num, 0, visited, solution, coll);
8:      return coll;
9: }
10:
11:  void GeneratePermute(vector<int> & num, int step,
12:      vector<int>& visited,
13:      vector<int>& solution,
14:      vector<vector<int> >& coll)
15: {
16:    if(step == num.size())
17:    {
18:        coll.push_back(solution);
19:        return;
20:    }
```

```
21:    for(int i =0; i< num.size(); i++)
22:    {
23:        if(visited[i] == 0)
24:        {
25:            visited[i] = 1;
26:            solution.push_back(num[i]);
27:            GeneratePermute(
28:                num, step+1, visited, solution, coll);
29:            solution.pop_back();
30:            visited[i] =0;
31:            while(i< num.size()-1 && num[i] == num[i+1])
32:                i++;
33:        }
34:    }
35: }
36:
```

76. Permutation Sequence

The set $[1,2,3,...,n]$ contains a total of $n!$ unique permutations.

By listing and labeling all of the permutations in order,

We get the following sequence (ie, for $n = 3$):

- "123"
- "132"
- "213"
- "231"
- "312"
- "321"

Given n and k, return the kth permutation sequence.

Note: Given n will be between 1 and 9 inclusive.

» Solve this problem

[Thoughts]
No one will doubt that this problem could be solved by DFS, like brute-force all possible permutation and return the kth. But obviously, this is not beauty enough.

Let's see how to solve it with math. Assume we have n digits in the input array, and the Kth permutation number is

$$a_1, \quad a_2, \quad a_3, \quad ..... \qquad ..., \quad a_n$$

if we igore a_1 for a while, and look at left n-1 digits first.

$$a_2, \quad a_3, \quad .... \quad .... \quad a_n$$

The count of n-1 digits permutations is (n-1)!. So, we can infer that

$$a_1 = K_1 / (n-1)! \quad K_1 = K$$

And same derivation could be apply to other digits. So we can get

$$a_2 = K_2 / (n-2)!$$
$$K_2 = K_1 \% (n-1)!$$
$$.......$$
$$a_{(n-1)} = K_{(n-1)} / 1!$$
$$K_{(n-1)} = K_{(n-2)} / 2!$$

```
an = K(n-1)
```

[Code]
```
1:  string getPermutation(int n, int k) {
2:      vector<int> nums(n);
3:      int permCount =1;
4:      for(int i =0; i< n; i++)
5:      {
6:          nums[i] = i+1;
7:          permCount *= (i+1);
8:      }
9:      // change K from (1,n) to (0, n-1) to accord to index
10:     k--;
11:     string targetNum;
12:     for(int i =0; i< n; i++)
13:     {
14:         permCount = permCount/ (n-i);
15:         int choosed = k / permCount;
16:         targetNum.push_back(nums[choosed] + '0');
17:         //restruct nums since one num has been picked
18:         for(int j =choosed; j< n-i; j++)
19:         {
20:             nums[j]=nums[j+1];
21:         }
22:         k = k%permCount;
23:     }
24:     return targetNum;
25: }
```

77. Plus One

Given a number represented as an array of digits, plus one to the number.
» Solve this problem

[Thoughts]
Simulate the add operation one digit by one and take proper care of the carry.

[Code]
```
1:  vector<int> plusOne(vector<int> &digits) {
2:      int cary=1, sum =0;
3:      vector<int> result(digits.size(),0);
4:      for(int i = digits.size()-1; i>=0; i--)
5:      {
6:          sum = cary+digits[i];
7:          cary = sum/10;
8:          result[i] = sum%10;
9:      }
10:     if(cary >0)
11:     {
12:         result.insert(result.begin(), cary);
13:     }
14:     return result;
15: }
16:
```

78. Populating Next Right Pointers in Each Node

Given a binary tree

```
struct TreeLinkNode {
    TreeLinkNode *left;
    TreeLinkNode *right;
    TreeLinkNode *next;
}
```

Populate each next pointer to point to its next right node. If there is no next right node, the next pointer should be set to NULL.
Initially, all next pointers are set to NULL.
Note:

- You may only use constant extra space.
- You may assume that it is a perfect binary tree (ie, all leaves are at the same level, and every parent has two children).

For example,
Given the following perfect binary tree,

```
        1
       / \
      2   3
     / \ / \
    4  5 6  7
```

After calling your function, the tree should look like:

```
         1 -> NULL
       / \
      2 -> 3 -> NULL
     / \ / \
    4->5->6->7 -> NULL
```

» Solve this problem

[Thoughts]

Notice that this problem gives a strict condition that this tree is a PERFECT binary tree. It simples the question a lot.
We can do it by recursion:

For each root node, for example node #2 in the sample
- link its left sub-node to right sub-node (4->5)

```
 2   ->   3 -> NULL
 / \      / \
4 -> 5 -> 6 -> 7 -> NULL
```

- link its right-sub node,
  - if root->next is not NULL, link to the left sub-node of root->next.(5->6)
  - If root->next is NULL, link to NULL.(7->NULL)

```
 2   ->   3 -> NULL
 / \      / \
4 -> 5 -> 6 -> 7 -> NULL
```

[Code]

```cpp
1:  void connect(TreeLinkNode *root) {
2:  // Start typing your C/C++ solution below
3:  // DO NOT write int main() function
4:  if(root == NULL) return;
5:  if(root->left != NULL)
6:      root->left->next = root->right;
7:  if(root->right !=NULL)
8:      root->right->next = root->next? root->next->left:NULL;
9:  connect(root->left);
10: connect(root->right);
11: }
```

79. Populating Next Right Pointers in Each Node II

Follow up for problem "*Populating Next Right Pointers in Each Node*".
What if the given tree could be any binary tree? Would your previous solution still work?
Note:

- You may only use constant extra space.

For example,
Given the following binary tree,

```
        1
       / \
      2   3
     / \   \
    4   5   7
```

After calling your function, the tree should look like:

```
        1 -> NULL
       / \
      2 -> 3 -> NULL
     / \     \
    4-> 5 -> 7 -> NULL
```

» Solve this problem

[Thoughts]
Similar as previous one. But this time, the tree is not guaranteed to be a complete binary tree. For each node, how to get the first valid node to be linked as next is the tricky part, e.g. node #6 in the sample is missed. So in order to link to #7, need to traverse all the parents nodes(#2, #3, NULL) and find the first node which has non-empty sub-node.

[Code]
```
1:  void connect(TreeLinkNode *root) {
2:     if(root== NULL) return;
```

```
3:      TreeLinkNode* p = root->next;
4:      while(p!=NULL)
5:      {
6:          if(p->left!=NULL)
7:          {
8:              p = p->left;
9:              break;
10:         }
11:         if(p->right!=NULL)
12:         {
13:             p = p->right;
14:             break;
15:         }
16:         p = p->next;
17:     }
18:     if(root->right!= NULL)
19:     {
20:         // link the right sub-node first
21:         root->right->next = p;
22:     }
23:     if(root->left !=NULL)
24:     {
25:         // then, link the left sub-node
26:         root->left->next = root->right? root->right:p;
27:     }
28:     connect(root->right);
29:     connect(root->left);
30: }
```

But unfortunately, previous solution problem requires constant space. Could we do this with O(1) space? Yes, see below:

```
1:      void connect(TreeLinkNode *root) {
2:          TreeLinkNode* cur = root, *next = NULL;
3:          while(cur!=NULL)
4:          {
```

```
5:          TreeLinkNode *p = cur, *k= NULL;
6:          while(p!=NULL)
7:          {
8:              TreeLinkNode* sub = getLinkedLeftNode(p);
9:              if(sub != NULL)
10:             {
11:                 if(next == NULL)
12:                 {
13:                     next = sub;
14:                     k = sub;
15:                 }
16:                 else
17:                     k->next = sub;
18:                 while(k->next !=NULL) // iterate to the tail
19:                     k = k->next;
20:             }
21:             p = p->next;
22:         }
23:         cur = next;
24:         next = NULL;
25:     }
26: }
27: TreeLinkNode* getLinkedLeftNode(TreeLinkNode * root)
28: {
29:     if(root->left != NULL && root->right != NULL)
30:         root->left->next = root->right;
31:     if(root->left != NULL)
32:         return root->left;
33:     if(root->right != NULL)
34:         return root->right;
35:     return NULL;
36: }
```

80. Recover Binary Search Tree

Two elements of a binary search tree (BST) are swapped by mistake.

Recover the tree without changing its structure.

Note:

A solution using O(*n*) space is pretty straight forward. Could you devise a constant space solution?

confused what "{1,#,2,3}" means? > read more on how binary tree is serialized on OJ.

» Solve this problem

[Thoughts]

This is a really interesting problem. One straight forward way is to do the inorder traverse of this binary search tree and then re-assign the value of each node. This solution is generic to N-swap mistakes.

Below is an example that shows how O(n) solution works.

```
1:  void recoverTree(TreeNode *root) {
2:      vector<TreeNode*> list;
3:      vector<int > vals;
4:      InOrderTravel(root, list, vals);
5:      sort(vals.begin(), vals.end());
6:      for(int i =0; i< list.size(); i++)
7:      {
8:          list[i]->val = vals[i];
9:      }
10: }
11: void InOrderTravel(TreeNode* node,
12:     vector<TreeNode*>& list, vector<int>& vals)
13: {
14:     if(node == NULL) return;
15:         InOrderTravel(node->left, list, vals);
16:     list.push_back(node);
17:     vals.push_back(node->val);
18:     InOrderTravel(node->right, list, vals);
```

```
19: }
```

But for this question, it only has two elements swapped by mistake and it ask for a O(1) space complexity. How to?

If we traverse this tree in order, actually, we can easily detect the the misplaced nodes during traversing. But inorder traversal always needs O(n) space because it needs a stack to track the path.

So here, the question becomes, could we travel the tree without any extral data struction like stack?
Fortunately, there is a solution Threaded Binary Tree. The general idea is, creating links to Inorder successor, traverse the tree using these links, and finally revert the changes to restore original tree.

```
1. Initialize current as root
2. While current is not NULL
     If current does not have left child
         a) Print current's data
         b) Go to the right, i.e., current =
current->right
     Else
         a) Make current as right child of the
rightmost node in current's left subtree
         b) Go to this left child, i.e.,
current = current->left
```

Following is the sample code of inorder traversal:

```
1: /* Function to traverse binary tree without recursion
2: and without stack */
3: vector<int> inorderTraversal(TreeNode *root)
4: {
5:     vector<int> result;
6:     TreeNode *current,*pre;
7:
8:     if(root == NULL)
```

```
9:      return result;
10:
11:     current = root;
12:     while(current != NULL)
13:     {
14:         if(current->left == NULL)
15:         {
16:             result.push_back(current->val);
17:             current = current->right;
18:         }
19:         else
20:         {
21:             /* Find the inorder predecessor of current */
22:             pre = current->left;
23:             while(pre->right != NULL
24:                     && pre->right != current)
25:                 pre = pre->right;
26:
27:             /* Make current as right child of
28:             its inorder predecessor */
29:             if(pre->right == NULL)
30:             {
31:                 pre->right = current;
32:                 current = current->left;
33:             }
34:
35:             /* Revert the changes made in if part to restore the
36:             original tree i.e., fix the right child of predecessor */
37:             else
38:             {
39:                 pre->right = NULL;
40:                 result.push_back(current->val);
41:                 current = current->right;
42:             } /* End of if condition pre->right == NULL */
43:         } /* End of if condition current->left == NULL*/
```

```
44:    } /* End of while */
45:
46:    return result;
47: }
48:
```

Based on threaded tree, we can use two pointers to travel the tree. Suppose, the pre pointer points the previous access node. The cur pointer points the current access node. Then, we can

Find first misplaced node by
if (current.val < prev.val)
  Node first = prev;

Find second misplaced node by
if (current.val < prev.val)
  Node second = current;

After traversal, swap the values of first and second node. Only need two pointers, prev and current node. O(1) space.

With all these information, we are done here. Traverse the tree with O(1) space and add the logic of resetting the misplaced nodes as a part of traversal logic.

[Code]

The change parts are highlight in red. Add an extra pointer to track the **predecessor node**. During traversing the tree, detect the misplaced node by (parent->val > current->val). And swap the parent node of first violation and the current node of second violation.

```
1:  void recoverTree(TreeNode *root)
2:  {
3:    TreeNode *f1=NULL, *f2=NULL;
4:    TreeNode *current,*pre, *parent=NULL;
5:
6:    if(root == NULL)
```

```
7:    return;
8:    bool found = false;
9:    current = root;
10:   while(current != NULL)
11:   {
12:       if(current->left == NULL)
13:       {
14:           if(parent && parent->val > current->val)
15:           {
16:               if(!found)
17:               {
18:                   f1 = parent;
19:                   found = true;
20:               }
21:               f2 = current;
22:           }
23:           parent = current;
24:           current = current->right;
25:       }
26:       else
27:       {
28:           /* Find the inorder predecessor of current */
29:           pre = current->left;
30:           while(pre->right != NULL
31:                   && pre->right != current)
32:               pre = pre->right;
33:
34:           /* Make current as right child of
35:           its inorder predecessor */
36:           if(pre->right == NULL)
37:           {
38:               pre->right = current;
39:               current = current->left;
40:           }
41:
```

```
42:              /* Revert the changes made in if part to restore the
43:              original tree i.e., fix the right child of predecssor */
44:         else
45:         {
46:            pre->right = NULL;
47:            if(parent->val > current->val)
48:            {
49:               if(!found)
50:               {
51:                  f1 = parent;
52:                  found = true;
53:               }
54:               f2 = current;
55:            }
56:            parent = current;
57:            current = current->right;
58:         } /* End of if condition pre->right == NULL */
59:      } /* End of if condition current->left == NULL*/
60:   } /* End of while */
61:
62:   if(f1 && f2)
63:   swap(f1->val, f2->val);
64: }
65:
```

81. Pow(x, n)

Implement pow(*x*, *n*).
» Solve this problem

[Thoughts]
Recursive bisection partitioning.
  If n is even, pow(x, n) = pow(x, n/2) * pow(x, n/2).
  If n is odd, pow(x, n) = pow(x, n/2) * pow(x, n/2) * x.
Just pay attention of the case n<0.

[Code]
```
1:  double power(double x, int n)
2:  {
3:      if (n == 0)
4:          return 1;
5:      double v = power(x, n / 2);
6:      if (n % 2 == 0)
7:          return v * v;
8:      else
9:          return v * v * x;
10: }
11: double pow(double x, int n) {
12:     if (n < 0)
13:         return 1.0 / power(x, -n);
14:     else
15:         return power(x, n);
16: }
```

82. Remove Duplicates from Sorted Array

Given a sorted array, remove the duplicates in place such that each element appear only *once* and return the new length.
Do not allocate extra space for another array, you must do this in place with constant memory.
For example,
Given input array A = [1,1,2],
Your function should return length = 2, and A is now [1,2].
» Solve this problem

[Thoughts]
This problem said SORTED array. This condition makes solution simpler. If the array is not sorted, we need either sort it first or track the frequency of occurrence via a map. Fortunately, we don't need to do too much work in this problem.

A classical two-pointer problem. Use two pointers to scan the array together. Because it is sorted, the first pointer can easily identify the duplicate by comparing the value with second pointer, and skip it. See code.

[Code]
```
1:  int removeDuplicates(int A[], int n) {
2:      if(n ==0) return 0;
3:      int index = 0;
4:      for(int i =0;i<n; i++)
5:      {
6:          if(A[index] == A[i]) // duplicate, skip
7:          {
8:              continue;
9:          }
10:         index++; // non-duplicate, copy it to second pointer
11:         A[index] = A[i];
12:     }
13:     return index+1;
```

```
14: }
```

83. Remove Duplicates from Sorted Array II

Follow up for "Remove Duplicates":
What if duplicates are allowed at most *twice*?
For example,
Given sorted array A = [1,1,1,2,2,3],
Your function should return length = 5, and A is
now [1,1,2,2,3].
» Solve this problem

[Thoughts]
Similar as previous problem. But need a variable to track the the frequency of occurrence during traversing. Again, if this array is not sorted, it's better to use a map.

[Code]
```
1:      int removeDuplicates(int A[], int n) {
2:          if(n == 0) return 0;
3:          int occur = 1;
4:          int index = 0;
5:          for(int i =1; i< n; i++)
6:          {
7:              if(A[index] == A[i])
8:              {
9:                  if(occur == 2)
10:                 {
11:                     continue;
12:                 }
13:                 occur++;
14:             }
15:             else
16:             {
17:                 occur =1 ;
18:             }
19:             A[++index] = A[i];
```

```
20:        }
21:        return index+1;
22:    }
```

84. Remove Duplicates from Sorted List

Given a sorted linked list, delete all duplicates such that each element appear only *once*.
For example,
Given 1->1->2, return 1->2.
Given 1->1->2->3->3, return 1->2->3.
» Solve this problem

[Thoughts]
Interesting transformation. Here, the problem is about linked list. Still use two-pointer, but this time, we need to deal with pointer operation.
One more important thing is, DELETE the unused node to avoid memory leak.

[Code]
```
1:  ListNode *deleteDuplicates(ListNode *head) {
2:     if(head == NULL) return NULL;
3:     ListNode * pre = head;
4:     ListNode *p = head->next;
5:     while(p!=NULL)
6:     {
7:        if(pre->val == p->val)
8:        {
9:           ListNode* temp = p;
10:          p = p->next;
11:          pre->next =p;
12:          // need delete the unused node. Or memory leak
13:          delete temp;
14:          continue;
15:       }
16:       pre = pre->next;
17:       p = p->next;
18:    }
```

```
19:    return head;
20: }
```

85. Remove Duplicates from Sorted List II

Given a sorted linked list, delete all nodes that have duplicate numbers, leaving only *distinct* numbers from the original list.
For example,
Given 1->2->3->3->4->4->5, return 1->2->5.
Given 1->1->1->2->3, return 2->3.
» Solve this problem

[Thoughts]
Add more tricks than previous problem. In previous problem, we need only delete the duplicate number. But in current one, we need to delete all the number which has duplicate. As above sample #2 {1->1->1->2->3}, we need to delete the head too. In order to avoid handling head node, I use a Safeguard (a fake head).

[Code]
```
1:  ListNode *deleteDuplicates(ListNode *head) {
2:     if(head == NULL) return head;
3:     ListNode *G = new ListNode(INT_MIN);
4:     G->next = head;
5:     ListNode *cur = G, *pre = head;
6:     while(pre!=NULL)
7:     {
8:         bool isDup = false;
9:         while(pre->next!=NULL
10:            && pre->val == pre->next->val)
11:        {
12:            isDup = true;
13:            ListNode *temp = pre;
14:            pre = pre->next;
15:            delete temp;
16:        }
17:        if(isDup)
18:        {
```

```
19:          ListNode *temp = pre;
20:          pre = pre->next;
21:          delete temp;
22:          continue;
23:      }
24:      cur->next = pre;
25:      cur = cur->next;
26:      pre= pre->next;
27:  }
28:  cur->next = pre;
29:  ListNode *temp = G->next;
30:  delete G;
31:  return temp;
32: }
33:
```

86. Remove Element

Given an array and a value, remove all instances of that value in place and return the new length.
The order of elements can be changed. It doesn't matter what you leave beyond the new length.
» Solve this problem

[Thoughts]
Use two pointers here. One pointer traverses the array and another pointer track the index of new string.
Suppose we are going to remove value N from array. If the first pointer points to a element which equals N too, skip it. If not, copy it to new address(second pointer).

[Code]

```
1:  int removeElement(int A[], int n, int elem) {
2:    int cur = 0;
3:    for(int i =0; i< n; i++)
4:    {
5:        if(A[i] == elem)
6:            continue;
7:        A[cur]=A[i];
8:        cur++;
9:    }
10:   return cur;
11: }
```

87. Remove Nth Node From End of List

Given a linked list, remove the nth node from the end of list and return its head.

For example,

> Given linked list: **1->2->3->4->5**, and **n = 2**.
>
> After removing the second node from the end, the linked list becomes **1->2->3->5**.

Note:

Given *n* will always be valid.

Try to do this in one pass.

» Solve this problem

[Thoughts]

A classical problem. Two pointers. One pointer moves n steps first, and then two pointers move together. When the first pointer arrives tail, the second pointer points exactly the node need to be deleted. As every linked list problem, head node always need more attention. E.g. 1->2->NULL, n =2; in this case, need delete the head node. Or, use a safe guard node to bypass head node trick.

[Code]

```
1:  ListNode *removeNthFromEnd(ListNode *head, int n) {
2:      ListNode* pre, *cur;
3:      pre = head;cur = head;
4:      int step = 0;
5:      while(step< n && cur!=NULL)
6:      {
7:          cur = cur->next;
8:          step++;
9:      }
10:     if(step ==n && cur == NULL)
11:     {
```

```
12:        head = head->next;
13:        delete pre;
14:        return head;
15:    }
16:    while(cur->next!=NULL)
17:    {
18:        pre = pre->next;
19:        cur = cur->next;
20:    }
21:    ListNode* temp = pre->next;
22:    pre->next = temp->next;
23:    delete temp;
24:    return head;
25: }
26:
```

88. Reorder List

Given a singly linked list $L: L_0 \rightarrow L_1 \rightarrow \ldots \rightarrow L_{n-1} \rightarrow L_n$,
reorder it to: $L_0 \rightarrow L_n \rightarrow L_1 \rightarrow L_{n-1} \rightarrow L_2 \rightarrow L_{n-2} \rightarrow \ldots$

You must do this in-place without altering the nodes' values.

For example,
Given {1,2,3,4}, reorder it to {1,4,2,3}.

[Thoughts]
For linked list problem, the "in-place" always means it expects
you to solve the problem via splitting and merging.

For this particular problem, we can solve it with 3 steps:
1. Use two pointers to traverse the list and find the middle
    node - N_m. Then cut the list into two lists by N_m. Here we
    call them as $L_{firsthalf}$ and $L_{secondhalf}$
2. Reverse the linked list $L_{secondhalf}$ and mark the new list as
    $L_{secondhalfreversed}$
3. Merge $L_{firsthalf}$ and $L_{secondhalfreversed}$ into a new list as the
    solution.

Besides Split & Merge, we can also solve this problem via
hashmap. For example, traverse the list once to get the length of
the list. With this length, we can pre-calculate the future index of
each node in the reordered list, and store the new index and
node mapping in the hashmap. In the end, traverse the hashmap
and relink the list.

Here I only provide the solution for Split & Merge, and leave the
hashmap one to the reader.

[Code]
```
1: void reorderList(ListNode *head) {
2:     if(head == NULL) return;
3:     // find the median node
4:     ListNode* fast = head;
5:     ListNode* slow = head;
```

```
6:     while(true)
7:     {
8:         fast = fast->next;
9:         if(fast == NULL)
10:            break;
11:        fast = fast->next;
12:        if(fast == NULL)
13:            break;
14:        slow = slow->next;
15:    }
16:    if(slow == NULL) return;
17:    // reverse second half of link list
18:    ListNode* cur = slow;
19:    ListNode* pre = slow->next;
20:    cur->next = NULL;
21:    while(pre!=NULL)
22:    {
23:        ListNode* temp = pre->next;
24:        pre->next = cur;
25:        cur = pre;
26:        pre = temp;
27:    }
28:    // merge two lists
29:    ListNode* first = head;
30:    ListNode* second = cur;
31:    while(second!= NULL&& first!=NULL && first!=second)
32:    {
33:        ListNode* temp = second->next;
34:        second->next = first->next;
35:        first->next = second;
36:        first = second->next;
37:        second = temp;
38:    }
39: }
```

89.   Restore IP Addresses

Given a string containing only digits, restore it by returning all possible valid IP address combinations.
For example:
Given `"25525511135"`,
return [`"255.255.11.135"`, `"255.255.111.35"`]. (Order does not matter)
» Solve this problem

[Thoughts]
Partition the given string into 4 parts and validate each part is in a correct range [0,255] and stands for a valid number, like "0.10.10.1" , not "0.10.010.1".
No difficulty here, but need more attention on implementation.

[Code]

```
1:    vector<string> restoreIpAddresses(string s) {
2:        vector<string> col;
3:        string ip;
4:        partitionIP(s, 0, 0, ip, col);
5:        return col;
6:    }
7:    void partitionIP(string s, int startIndex, int partNum,
8:    string resultIp, vector<string>& col)
9:    {
10:       //max: 3 bits per partition
11:       if(s.size() - startIndex > (4-partNum)*3) return;
12:       //min: 1 bit per partition
13:       if(s.size() - startIndex < (4-partNum)) return;
14:       if(startIndex == s.size() && partNum ==4)
15:       {
16:           resultIp.resize(resultIp.size()-1);
17:           col.push_back(resultIp);
18:           return;
19:       }
20:       int num =0;
```

```
21:        for(int i = startIndex; i< startIndex +3; i++)
22:        {
23:            num = num*10 + (s[i]-'0');
24:            if(num<=255)
25:            {
26:                resultIp+=s[i];
27:                partitionIP(s, i+1, partNum+1, resultIp+'.', col);
28:            }
29:            if(num ==0)//0.0.0.0 valid, but need to avoid
0.1.010.01
30:            {
31:                break;
32:            }
33:        }
34:    }
```

90.   Reverse Integer

Reverse digits of an integer.

Example1: x = 123, return 321

Example2: x = -123, return -321

click to show spoilers.
Have you thought about this?
Here are some good questions to ask before coding. Bonus points for you if you have already thought through this!
If the integer's last digit is 0, what should the output be? ie, cases such as 10, 100.
Did you notice that the reversed integer might overflow? Assume the input is a 32-bit integer, then the reverse of 1000000003 overflows. How should you handle such cases?
Throw an exception? Good, but what if throwing an exception is not an option? You would then have to re-design the function (ie, add an extra parameter).
» Solve this problem

[Thoughts]
You might think about converting the integer to string and reverse the string. But there are some special cases as '3000'. Zero needs special care in this case.

Actually, we don't need so complex solution. Just convert it as an integer.

[Code]
```
1:  int reverse(int x) {
2:      int newN =0, left =0;
3:      while(x != 0)
4:      {
5:          left = x%10;
6:          newN = newN*10 + left;
7:          x = x/10;
8:      }
9:      return newN;
```

```
10: }
11:
```

Previous code is beauty and brief. But it doesn't cover the overflow case. Below code only reverse the positive integer and detect the overflow if the integer becomes negative.

```
 1: int reverse(int x) {
 2:    int lastDigit = 0;
 3:    int result = 0;
 4:    bool isNeg = x>0? false:true;
 5:    x = abs(x);
 6:    while(x>0)
 7:    {
 8:        lastDigit = x%10;
 9:        result = result*10 + lastDigit;
10:        x = x/10;
11:    }
12:    if(result<0) return -1;
13:    if(isNeg)
14:        result *=-1;
15:    return result;
16: }
```

91. Reverse Linked List II

Reverse a linked list from position *m* to *n*. Do it in-place and in one-pass.

For example:

Given `1->2->3->4->5->NULL`, *m* = 2 and *n* = 4,

return `1->4->3->2->5->NULL`.

Note:

Given *m*, *n* satisfy the following condition:

1 ≤ *m* ≤ *n* ≤ length of list.

» Solve this problem

[Thoughts]

Split the solution into 3 steps:

1. Find the previous node of position m(Here, add a SafeGuard node to avoid handling head node)

2. Reverse the next N nodes after position m（two pointers:cur and post. cur always points to the head of reversed sub-list）

3. Merge the original linked list before position m, the reversed linked list between position m and position n, and also the left part linked list after position n.

This problem is a little tricky in implementation. Because it only ask for reverse a part of the original linked list, so you need to keep in mind that the whole list will be splitted into 3 part and you need to relink them together in the end.

[Code]

```
1:  ListNode *reverseBetween(ListNode *head, int m, int n) {
2:      int step = n-m;
3:      //intro a safe guard to avoid handle head case
4:      ListNode* safeG = new ListNode(-1);
5:      safeG->next = head;
6:      head = safeG;
7:      ListNode* pre = head;
8:      while(m>1)
9:      {
10:         pre=pre->next;
11:         m--;
```

```
12:     }
13:     ListNode* cur = pre->next, *post = cur->next;
14:     if(step>=1)
15:     {
16:         // Reverse the list after m
17:         while(step>0 && post!=NULL)
18:         {
19:             ListNode* temp = post->next;
20:             post->next = cur;
21:             cur = post;
22:             post = temp;
23:             step--;
24:         }
25:         // link the 3 lists together
26:         ListNode* temp = pre->next;
27:         pre->next = cur;
28:         temp->next = post;
29:     }
30:     safeG = head;  // remove safeG
31:     head = head->next;
32:     delete safeG;
33:     return head;
34: }
35:
```

92. Reverse Nodes in k-Group

Given a linked list, reverse the nodes of a linked list *k* at a time and return its modified list.

If the number of nodes is not a multiple of *k* then left-out nodes in the end should remain as it is.

You may not alter the values in the nodes, only nodes itself may be changed.

Only constant memory is allowed.

For example,

Given this linked list: 1->2->3->4->5

For *k* = 2, you should return: 2->1->4->3->5

For *k* = 3, you should return: 3->2->1->4->5

» Solve this problem

[Thoughts]

Similar as previous problem. Split the linked list into multiple K-groups. Apply the previous code for every K-group. The only trap is in the last group. If the nodes in last group is less than K, we don't need to reverse it. In the implementation, just reverse the tail again if it is less than K.

[Code]

The reverse code could be a separated function. But here, just put them together for readability.

```
1:  ListNode *reverseKGroup(ListNode *head, int k) {
2:      ListNode* safeG = new ListNode(-1);
3:      safeG->next = head;
4:      if(head == NULL || k==1) return head;
5:      ListNode* pre = safeG, *cur = head, *post = head->next;
6:      while(cur!=NULL)
7:      {
8:          post = cur->next;
9:          int i =0;
10:         while(i<k-1 && post!=NULL)
11:         {
12:             ListNode *temp = post->next;
13:             post->next = cur;
```

```
14:          cur = post;
15:          post = temp;
16:          i++;
17:     }
18:     if(i!=k-1)
19:     {
20:          int k =0;
21:          ListNode * temp = post;
22:          post = cur;
23:          cur = temp;
24:          while(k<i)
25:          {
26:              temp = post->next;
27:              post->next = cur;
28:              cur = post;
29:              post = temp;
30:              k++;
31:          }
32:          break;
33:     }
34:     ListNode* temp = pre->next;
35:     pre->next = cur;
36:     temp->next = post;
37:     pre = temp;
38:     cur = pre->next;
39: }
40: head = safeG->next;
41: delete safeG;
42: return head;
43: }
44:
```

93. Roman To Integer

Given a roman numeral, convert it to an integer.

Input is guaranteed to be within the range from 1 to 3999.

» Solve this problem

[Thoughts]

First, we need an static array or function to map the roman number to integer. Then, scan the roman string from left to right,

- if current roman number is larger than previous, it means these two numbers are combo number. The correct value should be current number minus previous one, e.g. IV = 5-1
- else, add current roman number into integer result and process next number. e.g. VI=5+1, II = 1+1

[Code]

```
1:  inline int c2n(char c) {
2:     switch(c) {
3:        case 'I': return 1;
4:        case 'V': return 5;
5:        case 'X': return 10;
6:        case 'L': return 50;
7:        case 'C': return 100;
8:        case 'D': return 500;
9:        case 'M': return 1000;
10:       default: return 0;
11:    }
12: }
13:
14: int romanToInt(string s) {
15:    int result=0;
16:    for(int i =0; i< s.size(); i++)
17:    {
18:        if(i>0&& c2n(s[i]) > c2n(s[i-1]))
19:        {
20:            result +=(c2n(s[i]) - 2*c2n(s[i-1]));
```

```
21:        }
22:        else
23:        {
24:            result += c2n(s[i]);
25:        }
26:    }
27:    return result;
28: }
```

94. Rotate Image

You are given an *n* x *n* 2D matrix representing an image.
Rotate the image by 90 degrees (clockwise).
Follow up:
Could you do this in-place?
» Solve this problem

[Thoughts]
As below, first, rotate the image by diagonal. And then rotate it
by the median line of y-axis.

$$\begin{matrix} 1, & 2 \\ 3, & 4 \end{matrix} \implies \begin{matrix} 4, & 2 \\ 3, & 1 \end{matrix} \implies \begin{matrix} 3, & 1 \\ 4, & 2 \end{matrix}$$

[Code]

```
1:  void rotate(vector<vector<int> > &matrix) {
2:      int len = matrix[0].size();
3:      for(int i =0; i<len-1; i++)
4:      {
5:          for(int j=0;j<len-i;j++)
6:          {
7:              swap(matrix[i][j], matrix[len-1-j][len-1-i]);
8:          }
9:      }
10:     for(int i =0; i<len/2; i++)
11:     {
12:         for(int j=0;j<len;j++)
13:         {
14:             swap(matrix[i][j], matrix[len-i-1][j]);
15:         }
16:     }
17: }
18: void swap(int& a1, int&a2)
19: {
20:     int temp = a1;
```

```
21:     a1=a2;
22:     a2=temp;
23: }
```

95. Rotate List

Given a list, rotate the list to the right by *k* places, where *k* is non-negative.
For example:
Given 1->2->3->4->5->NULL and *k* = 2,
return 4->5->1->2->3->NULL.
» Solve this problem

[Thoughts]
Interesting problem.
1.   scan from head to tail and get the length of linked list
2.   Link tail to head and form a ring.
3.   Continue to move forward for another (len – k%len) nodes
4.   Break the ring, and done.

[Code]
```
1:  ListNode *rotateRight(ListNode *head, int k) {
2:      if(head == NULL || k ==0) return head;
3:      int len =1;
4:      ListNode* p = head,*pre;
5:      while(p->next!=NULL)
6:      {
7:          p = p->next;
8:          len++;
9:      }
10:     k = len-k%len;
11:     p->next = head;
12:     int step =0;
13:     while(step< k)
14:     {
15:         p = p->next;
16:         step++;
17:     }
18:     head = p->next;
19:     p->next = NULL;
```

```
20:     return head;
21: }
```

[Note]

K might be larger than len. So here, need to use (K mod len).

96. Scramble String

Given a string *s1*, we may represent it as a binary tree by partitioning it to two non-empty substrings recursively. Below is one possible representation of *s1* = `"great"`:

```
      great
     /     \
   gr      eat
  / \     /   \
 g   r   e    at
             /  \
            a    t
```

To scramble the string, we may choose any non-leaf node and swap its two children.
For example, if we choose the node `"gr"` and swap its two children, it produces a scrambled string `"rgeat"`.

```
      rgeat
     /     \
   rg      eat
  / \     /   \
 r   g   e    at
             /  \
            a    t
```

We say that `"rgeat"` is a scrambled string of `"great"`.
Similarly, if we continue to swap the children of nodes `"eat"` and `"at"`, it produces a scrambled string `"rgtae"`.

```
      rgtae
     /     \
   rg      tae
  / \     /   \
 r   g   ta    e
         /  \
        t    a
```

We say that `"rgtae"` is a scrambled string of `"great"`.

Given two strings *s1* and *s2* of the same length, determine if *s2* is a scrambled string of *s1*.
» Solve this problem

[Thoughts]
Definitely, we can use recursion. Partition two string to 4 parts, and compare the four groups: (A.left, B.left) && (A.right, B.right), (A.left, B.right) && (A.right, B.left). But recursion usually is not efficient especially when the data set is large. So, need some pruning to cut unnecessary computing.
There should be a O(n) solution. Still thinking.

[Code]
```
1:   bool isScramble(string s1, string s2) {
2:      if(s1.size() != s2.size()) return false;
3:      int A[26];
4:      memset(A,0,26*sizeof(A[0]));
5:      for(int i =0;i<s1.size(); i++)
6:      {
7:          A[s1[i]-'a']++;
8:      }
9:      for(int i =0;i<s2.size(); i++)
10:     {
11:         A[s2[i]-'a']--;
12:     }
13:     for(int i =0;i<26; i++)
14:     {
15:         if(A[i] !=0)
16:             return false;
17:     }
18:     if(s1.size() ==1 && s2.size() ==1) return true;
19:     for(int i =1; i< s1.size(); i++)
20:     {
21:
22:         bool result=
23:             isScramble(
```

```
24:            s1.substr(0, i),
25:            s2.substr(0, i))
26:         && isScramble(
27:            s1.substr(i, s1.size()-i),
28:            s2.substr(i, s1.size()-i));
29:       result = result
30:       || (isScramble(
31:            s1.substr(0, i),
32:            s2.substr(s2.size() - i, i))
33:         && isScramble(
34:            s1.substr(i, s1.size()-i),
35:            s2.substr(0, s1.size()-i)));
36:       if(result) return true;
37:    }
38:    return false;
39: }
```

97. Search a 2D Matrix

Write an efficient algorithm that searches for a value in an *m* x *n* matrix. This matrix has the following properties:

- Integers in each row are sorted from left to right.
- The first integer of each row is greater than the last integer of the previous row.

For example,

Consider the following matrix:

```
[
    [1,    3,   5,   7],
    [10,  11,  16,  20],
    [23,  30,  34,  50]
]
```

Given **target** = 3, return `true`.
» Solve this problem

[Thoughts]
There are two ways to solve this problem.

Solution #1. Do the binary search twice. Use the first binary search to identify which row the target might sit. And apply the second binary search on the row selected in the first round search and find the index of the target if it exists in this row,

Solution #2. Forget this is a matrix. Just flat it to a one-dimensional array, like [1, 3, 5, 7, 10, 11, 16, 20, 23, 30, 34, 50]. And apply the binary search on this one-dimensional array. The only trick here is to convert the index from one-dimension to two-dimension, for example, the ith element is one-dimension array indicate the index (i/n, i%n☐) in the matrix.

Here provide the code for solution #1, and leave the solution #2 to reader.

[Code]

```
1:  bool searchMatrix(vector<vector<int> > &matrix, int target) {
2:     int row = matrix.size();
3:     if(row ==0) return false;
4:     int col = matrix[0].size();
5:     if(col ==0) return false;
6:     if(target< matrix[0][0]) return false;
7:     int start = 0, end = row-1;
8:     while(start<= end)
9:     {
10:        int mid = (start+end)/2;
11:        if(matrix[mid][0] == target)
12:           return true;
13:        else if(matrix[mid][0] < target)
14:           start = mid+1;
15:        else
16:           end = mid-1;
17:     }
18:     int targetRow = end;
19:     start =0;
20:     end = col-1;
21:     while(start <=end)
22:     {
23:        int mid = (start+end)/2;
24:        if(matrix[targetRow][mid] == target)
25:           return true;
26:        else if(matrix[targetRow][mid] < target)
27:           start = mid+1;
28:        else
29:           end = mid-1;
30:     }
31:     return false;
32: }
```

98.   Search for a Range

Given a sorted array of integers, find the starting and ending position of a given target value.
Your algorithm's runtime complexity must be in the order of O(log *n*).
If the target is not found in the array, return [-1, -1].
For example,
Given [5, 7, 7, 8, 8, 10] and target value 8,
return [3, 4].
» Solve this problem

[Thoughts]
Do binary search twice. The first one is to find the left boundary, the second is to find the right boundary. So the average complexity is O(lgn).

[Code]
```
1:  vector<int> searchRange(int A[], int n, int target) {
2:      vector<int> result;
3:      result.push_back(-1);
4:      result.push_back(-1);
5:      // find the low bound of the range, O(lgn)
6:      int start =0, end =n-1;
7:      while(start < end)
8:      {
9:          int mid = (start + end)/2;
10:          if(A[mid] < target)
11:          {
12:              start = mid + 1;
13:              continue;
14:          }
15:          end = mid;
16:      }
17:      int low_bound = A[start] == target? start:-1;
18:      if(low_bound == -1)
```

```
19:    {
20:       return result;
21:    }
22:    // find the high bound of the range, O(lgn)
23:    start =low_bound, end =n;
24:    while(start < end)
25:    {
26:       int mid = (start + end)/2;
27:       if(A[mid] > target)
28:       {
29:          end = mid;
30:          continue;
31:       }
32:       start = mid+1;
33:    }
34:    int high_bound = start-1;
35:    result.clear();
36:    result.push_back(low_bound);
37:    result.push_back(high_bound);
38:    return result;
39: }
```

99. Search in Rotated Sorted Array

Suppose a sorted array is rotated at some pivot unknown to you
beforehand.
(i.e., 0 1 2 4 5 6 7 might become 4 5 6 7 0 1 2).
You are given a target value to search. If found in the array
return its index, otherwise return -1.
You may assume no duplicate exists in the array.
» Solve this problem

[Thoughts]
Binary search. But need to pay more attention on the boundary
of rotated part. Need two inequalities to judge:
1. A[m] ? A[left]
2. A[m] ? target
See the judging logic in code.

[Code]
```
1:  int search(int A[], int n, int target) {
2:      int l = 0, r = n-1;
3:      while(l<=r)
4:      {
5:          int m = (l+r)/2;
6:          if(A[m] == target) return m;
7:          if(A[m]>= A[l])
8:          {
9:              // target 5 in {4,5,6,2,3}
10:             if(A[l]<=target && target<= A[m])
11:                 r=m-1;
12:             else
13:                 l = m+1;
14:         }
15:         else
16:         {
17:             // target 2 in {5,0,1,2,3}
18:             if(A[m] < target && target< A[l])
19:                 l = m+1;
```

```
20:          else
21:               r = m-1;
22:          }
23:     }
24:     return -1;
25: }
```

100. Search in Rotated Sorted Array II

Follow up for "Search in Rotated Sorted Array":
What if *duplicates* are allowed?
Would this affect the run-time complexity? How and why?
Write a function to determine if a given target is in the array.
» Solve this problem

[Thoughts]
Yes, duplicates will impact the run-time complexity. In worst case, it will use O(n) to find the target, like {1,1,1,1,5,1}. In previous solution, we use A[m]>=A[l] to detect whether [l,m] is an increasing sequence, but now this assumption is not true any more, e.g. [1,3,1,1,1].

So in order to keep our assumption, we need to split previous inequality into two parts:
1. if A[m]>A[l], [l,m] is increasing sequence.
2. if A[m] ==A[l], no decision. So move forward one step(l++) and see.

[Code]
```
1:      bool search(int A[], int n, int target) {
2:          int start = 0;
3:          int end = n-1;
4:          while(start <= end)
5:          {
6:              int mid = (start+end)/2;
7:              if(A[mid] == target) return true;
8:              if(A[start] < A[mid])
9:              {
10:                 if(target>=A[start] && target<A[mid])
11:                     end = mid-1;
12:                 else
13:                     start = mid+1;
14:             }
15:             else if(A[start] > A[mid])
16:             {
```

```
17:              if(target>A[mid] && target<=A[end])
18:                  start = mid+1;
19:              else
20:                  end = mid-1;
21:          }
22:          else //skip duplicate one, A[start] == A[mid]
23:              start++;
24:      }
25:      return false;
26:  }
```

101. Search Insert Position

Given a sorted array and a target value, return the index if the target is found. If not, return the index where it would be if it were inserted in order.
You may assume no duplicates in the array.
Here are few examples.
[1,3,5,6], 5 → 2
[1,3,5,6], 2 → 1
[1,3,5,6], 7 → 4
[1,3,5,6], 0 → 0
» Solve this problem

[Thoughts]
Similar as classic binary search, only one line difference(as Line 7,8) to determine the insert index.

[Code]
```
1:  int searchInsert(int A[], int n, int target) {
2:      int l=0, r=n-1;
3:      while(l<=r)
4:      {
5:          int mid = (l+r)/2;
6:          if(A[mid] == target) return mid;
7:          if(mid>l && A[mid]>target && A[mid-1]<target )
8:              return mid;
9:          if(A[mid] > target)
10:              r= mid-1;
11:         else
12:              l=mid+1;
13:     }
14:     return l;
15: }
```

102. Serialize and De-serialize a tree

A very frequent interview question. Suppose you have a tree, how could you serialize it to file and revert it back?
for example,

[Thoughts]
The most obvious and simple way is taking advantage of pre-order traversal. If we mark the NULL node as "#", the example in the problem description could be represented as below.

If we do the pre-order traverse on this tree by using following code,

```
1:  void Serialize(TreeNode * node, vector<char> &output)
2:  {
3:      if(node == NULL)
4:      {
5:          output.push_back('#');
6:          return;
7:      }
8:      output.push_back(node->val + '0');
9:      Serialize(node->left, output);
10:     Serialize(node->right, output);
```

```
11: }
```

The pre-order traversal result will be
{'1','2','#','4','6','#','#','7','#','#','3','5','#','#','#'};

The next question is, how could recover the tree via this string?
Similar, run the pre-prder again on the traversal result this time
as below:

```
1:  TreeNode *Deserialize(vector<char> output, int &index)
2:  {
3:      if(index > output.size()
4:             || output[index] == '#') return NULL;
5:      TreeNode *node = new TreeNode(output[index] -'0');
6:      index ++;
7:      node->left = Deserialize(output, index);
8:      index++;
9:      node->right = Deserialize(output, index);
10:     return node;
11: }
```

And here is questions for you. Is it possible to serialize and de-
serialize the tree via in-order traversal? How about post-order
traversal? Or traverse the tree in level order?

103. Set Matrix Zeroes

Given a *m* x *n* matrix, if an element is 0, set its entire row and column to 0. Do it in place.
Follow up:
Did you use extra space?
A straight forward solution using O(mn) space is probably a bad idea.
A simple improvement uses O($m + n$) space, but still not the best solution.
Could you devise a constant space solution?
» Solve this problem

[Thoughts]
A quit boring problem. The tricky part is how to store the flag bits. One way is to create a O(m+n) array, but this problem asks to use constant space. So the best way is to reuse the existing array. For example, to use the first row and first column to store the flg bits like below:

1. Check whether the first row and first column need to be cleaned or not.
2. Scan the left matrix, if meets 0, set the flag bit in first row and first column
3. Rescan the matrix. Clean the matrix based on the flg bit in first row and first column
4. Clean first row and first column based on #1 result.

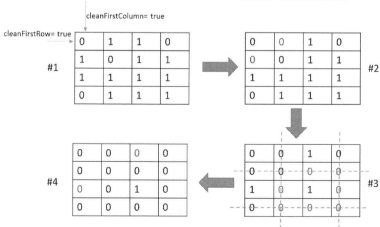

[Code]

```
1:  void setZeroes(vector<vector<int> > &matrix) {
2:      assert(matrix.size()>0);
3:      int row = matrix.size(), col = matrix[0].size();
4:      bool zerorow=false, zerocol=false;
5:      for(int i = 0; i< col; i++)
6:          if(matrix[0][i] ==0)
7:              zerorow = 1;
8:      for(int i = 0; i< row; i++)
9:          if(matrix[i][0] ==0)
10:             zerocol=1;
11:     for(int i =1; i < row; i++)
12:         for(int j = 1; j<col; j++)
13:             if(matrix[i][j] ==0)
14:             {
15:                 matrix[0][j] =0;
16:                 matrix[i][0] =0;
17:             }
18:     for(int i =1; i < row; i++)
19:         for(int j = 1; j<col; j++)
20:             if(matrix[i][0] ==0 || matrix[0][j] ==0)
21:                 matrix[i][j] =0;
22:     if(zerorow ==1)
23:         for(int i =0; i< col; i++)
24:             matrix[0][i] =0;
25:     if(zerocol==1)
26:         for(int i =0; i< row; i++)
27:             matrix[i][0] =0;
28: }
```

104. Simplify Path

Given an absolute path for a file (Unix-style), simplify it.
For example,
path = `"/home/"`, => `"/home"`
path = `"/a/./b/../../c/"`, => `"/c"`
Corner Cases:

- Did you consider the case where **path** = `"/../"`?
  In this case, you should return `"/"`.
- Another corner case is the path might contain multiple
  slashes `'/'` together, such as `"/home//foo/"`.
  In this case, you should ignore redundant slashes and
  return `"/home/foo"`.

» Solve this problem

[Thoughts]
Take the advantage of the stack, if next string element
- Equals "/" , skip and find the next element
- Equals "." , do nothing and find the next element
- Equals ".." , pop the top element in stack, and find the
  next element
- Equals other else, push the element into stack , and find
  the next element

And finally, reconstruct the path by stack. Using stack will need
extra space, but it saves the complexity of tracking the element
index, like multiple "/../"

[Code]
```
1:  string simplifyPath(string path) {
2:      vector<string> stack;
3:      assert(path[0]=='/');
4:      int i=0;
5:      while(i< path.size())
6:      {
7:          //skip the begining '////'
8:          while(path[i] =='/' && i< path.size()) i++;
```

```
9:      if(i == path.size())
10:         break;
11:       int start = i;
12:       //decide the end boundary
13:       while(path[i]!='/' && i< path.size()) i++;
14:       int end = i-1;
15:       string element = path.substr(start, end-start+1);
16:       if(element == "..")
17:       {
18:          if(stack.size() >0)
19:              stack.pop_back();
20:       }
21:       else if(element!=".")
22:            stack.push_back(element);
23:    }
24:    if(stack.size() ==0) return "/";
25:    string simpPath;
26:    for(int i =0; i<stack.size(); i++)
27:        simpPath += "/" + stack[i];
28:    return simpPath;
29: }
```

105. Single Number

Given an array of integers, every element appears *twice* except for one. Find that single one.
Note:
Your algorithm should have a linear runtime complexity. Could you implement it without using extra memory?

[Thoughts]
This problem tests the bit operation. From the problem description, we need to filter all the elements which appears twice and the left number is the single number.

As in bit operations, for eliminating the duplicate, the most straightforward way is to use Exclusive Or. For any two numbers with same value, the result of their Exclusive Or is ZERO.

So, we get the solution. Iterate the array once, and keep do the Exclusive Or on every number. And the left value is the single number this problem asks for.

[Code]
```
1: int singleNumber(int A[], int n) {
2:     int left = A[0];
3:     for(int i =1; i< n; i++)
4:     {
5:         left = left ^ A[i];
6:     }
7:     return left;
8: }
```

106. Single Number II

Given an array of integers, every element appears *three* times except for one. Find that single one.

Note:
Your algorithm should have a linear runtime complexity. Could you implement it without using extra memory?

[Thoughts]
Similar as previous "Single Number", this problem also has mathematical solution via bit operation. If you are interested in the math, you can google it in the internet.

Here, let's look at a generic solution. As the first step, let's assume there is no single number in the array and every element appears 3 time. And for each integer, it has 32 bits in the binary format. If we do the calculation on the bits, for example sum up the 1's count, it's easy to know that the count of 1 in each bit should be a multiple of 3.

So the solution is, iterate the array once and count the 1 in each bit of the element. After that, mod the count of each bit by 3. The left value is the single number.

[Code]
```
1: int singleNumber(int A[], int n) {
2:     vector<int> bit(32,0);
3:     for(int i =0; i< n; ++i)
4:     {
5:         int k=1;
6:         for(int j =0; j<32; ++j)
7:         {
8:             int rotated;
9:             if((rotated = A[i]>>j) == 0) break;
10:            bit[j] += rotated & k;
11:        }
12:    }
```

```
13:     int target=0;
14:     for(int i =0; i<32; ++i)
15:     {
16:         target += (bit[i]%3 <<i);
17:     }
18:     return target;
19: }
```

107. Sort Colors

Given an array with *n* objects colored red, white or blue, sort them so that objects of the same color are adjacent, with the colors in the order red, white and blue.
Here, we will use the integers 0, 1, and 2 to represent the color red, white, and blue respectively.

Note:
You are not suppose to use the library's sort function for this problem.

Follow up:
A rather straight forward solution is a two-pass algorithm using counting sort.
First, iterate the array counting number of 0's, 1's, and 2's, then overwrite array with total number of 0's, then 1's and followed by 2's.
Could you come up with an one-pass algorithm using only constant space?
» Solve this problem

[Thoughts]
A very straight forward way is to use counting sort, but counting sort needs two round scan. The first round is to count the number of red, white and blue. And the second round will generat the new array based on the statistic info from the first round scan.

But this problem requires only one pass. So, use two-pointer to track two 'index' here. One for red, one for blue. Narrow down the index from both sides to middle.

$redIndex=0
$blueIndex=N-1
San array[i] from 0 to N-1,
- If meets 0, swap it with red index, and $redIndex ++
- If meets 2, swap it with blue index, and $blueIndex - -
- If meets 1, i++

One pass scan. Time complexity O(n), space complexity O(1).

[Code]

```
1:     void sortColors(int A[], int n) {
2:         // Start typing your C/C++ solution below
3:         // DO NOT write int main() function
4:         int redSt=0, bluSt=n-1;
5:         int i=0;
6:         while(i<bluSt+1)
7:         {
8:             if(A[i]==0)
9:             {
10:                 std::swap(A[i],A[redSt]);
11:                 redSt++;
12:                 i++;  //move scan index together with red index
13:                 continue;
14:             }
15:             if(A[i] ==2)
16:             {
17:                 std::swap(A[i],A[bluSt]);
18:                 bluSt--;  //only move blue index
19:                 continue;
20:             }
21:             i++;
22:         }
23:     }
```

[Note]
Line 12, move the scan index because we scan the array from left to right. But if we scan the array from right to left, need to move the scan index in Line 19 instead of Line 12.

108. Sort List

Sort a linked list in $O(n \log n)$ time using constant space complexity.

[Thoughts]
When we say the O(nlgn) sort algrithom, most of the time, we are making the discussion among quick sort, merge sort, heap sort etc.

Here the solution is using the same idea of merge sort. One example as below:

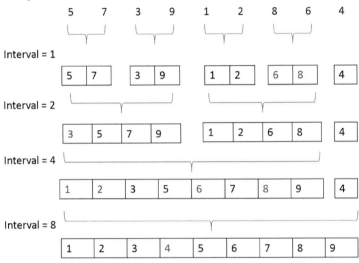

For each round, the merge iteration is O(n). And for merge sort, we totally need run the iteration for lg(n) round(the height of recursion tree). So, the total time complexity is O(nlgn).

[Code]

```
1:  ListNode *sortList(ListNode *head) {
2:      // Get length first
3:      ListNode* p = head;
4:      int len = 0;
5:      while (p != NULL)
6:      {
7:          p = p->next;
```

```
8:        len++;
9:    }
10:    ListNode* fakehead = new ListNode(-1);
11:    fakehead->next = head;
12:    for (int interval = 1; interval <= len; interval = interval * 2)
13:    {
14:       ListNode* pre = fakehead;
15:       ListNode* slow = fakehead->next,
16:              *fast = fakehead->next;
17:       while (fast != NULL || slow != NULL)
18:       {
19:          int i = 0;
20:          while (i< interval && fast != NULL)
21:          {
22:             //move fast pointer ahead 'interval' steps
23:             fast = fast->next;
24:             i++;
25:          }
26:          //merge two lists, each has 'interval' length
27:          int fvisit = 0, svisit = 0;
28:          while (fvisit < interval
29:             && svisit<interval
30:             && fast != NULL && slow != NULL)
31:          {
32:             if (fast->val < slow->val)
33:             {
34:                pre->next = fast;
35:                pre = fast;
36:                fast = fast->next;
37:                fvisit++;
38:             }
39:             else
40:             {
41:                pre->next = slow;
42:                pre = slow;
```

```
43:                    slow = slow->next;
44:                        svisit++;
45:                    }
46:                }
47:                while (fvisit < interval && fast != NULL)
48:                {
49:                    pre->next = fast;
50:                    pre = fast;
51:                    fast = fast->next;
52:                    fvisit++;
53:                }
54:                while (svisit < interval && slow != NULL)
55:                {
56:                    pre->next = slow;
57:                    pre = slow;
58:                    slow = slow->next;
59:                    svisit++;
60:                }
61:                pre->next = fast;
62:                slow = fast;
63:            }
64:        }
65:    ListNode* newhead = fakehead->next;
66:    delete fakehead;
67:    return newhead;
68: }
69:
```

109. Spiral Matrix

Given a matrix of *m* x *n* elements (*m* rows, *n* columns), return all elements of the matrix in spiral order.

For example,

Given the following matrix:

```
[
  [ 1,  2,  3 ],
  [ 4,  5,  6 ],
  [ 7,  8,  9 ]
]
```

You should return [1,2,3,6,9,8,7,4,5].
» Solve this problem

[Thoughts]
An implementation, which need to be careful of handling 4 directions. See code part.

[Code]

```
1:  vector<int> spiralOrder(vector<vector<int> > &matrix) {
2:      vector<int> output;
3:      int row_len = matrix.size();
4:      if(row_len ==0) return output;
5:      int col_len = matrix[0].size();
6:      print_order(matrix, 0, row_len, 0, col_len, output);
7:      return output;
8:  }
9:  void print_order(
10:     vector<vector<int> > &matrix,
11:     int row_s, int row_len,
12:     int col_s, int col_len,
13:     vector<int>& output)
14:  {
```

```
15:    if(row_len<=0 || col_len <=0) return;
16:    if(row_len ==1)
17:    {
18:        for(int i =col_s; i< col_s+col_len; i++)
19:            output.push_back(matrix[row_s][i]);
20:        return;
21:    }
22:    if(col_len ==1)
23:    {
24:        for(int i =row_s; i<row_s + row_len; i++)
25:            output.push_back(matrix[i][col_s]);
26:        return;
27:    }
28:    for(int i =col_s; i<col_s+col_len-1; i++) //up
29:        output.push_back(matrix[row_s][i]);
30:    for(int i =row_s; i<row_s+row_len-1; i++)  //right
31:        output.push_back(matrix[i][col_s+col_len-1]);
32:    for(int i =col_s; i<col_s+col_len-1; i++) //bottom
33:        output.push_back(
34:            matrix[row_s+row_len-1][2*col_s+ col_len-1 -i]);
35:    for(int i =row_s; i<row_s+row_len-1; i++) //left
36:        output.push_back(
37:            matrix[2*row_s+row_len-1-i][col_s]);
38:    print_order( matrix, row_s+1, row_len-2,
39:            col_s+1, col_len-2, output);
40: }
```

Another implementation without using recursion. This version is a bit easy to read.

```
1: vector<int> spiralOrder(vector<vector<int> > &matrix) {
2:     vector<int> result;
3:     int row = matrix.size();
4:     if(row == 0) return result;
5:     int col = matrix[0].size();
```

```
6:    if(col == 0) return result;
7:    //define the step for 4 directions
8:    int x[4] = { 1, 0, -1, 0 };
9:    int y[4] = { 0, 1, 0, -1 };
10:   int visitedRows = 0;
11:   int visitedCols = 0;
12:   // define direction:
13:   // 0 means up, 1 means down, 2 means left, 3 means right
14:   int direction = 0;
15:   int startx = 0, starty = 0;
16:   int candidateNum = 0, moveStep = 0;
17:   while (true)
18:   {
19:       if (x[direction] == 0) // visit y axis
20:           candidateNum = row - visitedRows;
21:       else // visit x axis
22:           candidateNum = col - visitedCols;
23:       if (candidateNum <= 0)
24:           break;
25:       result.push_back(matrix[starty][startx]);
26:       moveStep++;
27:       if (candidateNum == moveStep) // change direction
28:       {
29:           visitedRows += x[direction] == 0 ? 0 : 1;
30:           visitedCols += y[direction] == 0 ? 0 : 1;
31:           direction = (direction + 1) % 4;
32:           moveStep = 0;
33:       }
34:       startx += x[direction];
35:       starty += y[direction];
36:   }
37:   return result;
38: }
```

110. Spiral Matrix II

Given an integer *n*, generate a square matrix filled with elements from 1 to n^2 in spiral order.

For example,

Given *n* = 3,
You should return the following matrix:

```
[
  [ 1,  2,  3 ],
  [ 8,  9,  4 ],
  [ 7,  6,  5 ]
]
```

» Solve this problem

[Thoughts]
Similar as previous "Spriral Matrix". Here use recursion to build the matrix.

[Code]
Comparing with the code of "Spriral Matrix", the differences are marked by underline.

```
1:  vector<vector<int> > generateMatrix(int n) {
2:      vector<vector<int>> matrix(n);
3:      for(int i =0; i< n; i++)
4:      {
5:          matrix[i].resize(n);
6:      }
7:      generate_order(matrix, 0, n, 0, n, 1);
8:      return matrix;
9: }
10: void generate_order(
11:     vector<vector<int> > &matrix,
12:     int row_s, int row_len,
13:     int col_s, int col_len,
```

```
14:    int val)
15:    {
16:        if(row_len<=0 || col_len <=0) return;
17:        if(row_len ==1)
18:        {
19:            for(int i =col_s; i< col_s+col_len; i++)
20:                matrix[row_s][i] = val++;
21:            return;
22:        }
23:        if(col_len ==1)
24:        {
25:            for(int i =row_s; i<row_s + row_len; i++)
26:                matrix[i][col_s] = val++;
27:            return;
28:        }
29:        for(int i =col_s; i<col_s+col_len-1; i++) //up
30:            matrix[row_s][i] = val++;
31:        for(int i =row_s; i<row_s+row_len-1; i++) //right
32:            matrix[i][col_s+col_len-1] = val++;
33:        for(int i =col_s; i<col_s+col_len-1; i++) //bottom
34:            matrix[row_s+row_len-1][2*col_s+ col_len-1 -i]
35:                = val++;
36:        for(int i =row_s; i<row_s+row_len-1; i++) //left
37:            matrix[2*row_s+row_len-1-i][col_s] = val++;
38:        generate_order( matrix, row_s+1, row_len-2,
39:                        col_s+1, col_len-2, val);
40: }
```

111. Sqrt(x)

Implement `int sqrt(int x)`.

Compute and return the square root of *x*.
» Solve this problem

[Thoughts]
Not an interesting problem, but a good example to show binary search. The one tricky here is how to determine the end boundary of binary search. The multiply operation may cause integer overflow. So it's hard to decide the end by comparing the value with 0. A good way is to using a fixed end boundary, like sqrt(INT_MAX).

[Code]
```
1:  int sqrt(int x) {
2:      int start =0, end;
3:      end= x/2<std::sqrt(INT_MAX)?
4:              x/2+1:std::sqrt(INT_MAX);
5:      while(start<= end)
6:      {
7:          int mid = (start+end)/2;
8:          int sqr = mid*mid;
9:          if(sqr ==x)
10:         {
11:             return mid;
12:         }
13:         if(sqr<x)
14:         {
15:             start = mid+1;
16:         }
17:         else
18:         {
19:             end = mid-1;
20:         }
21:     }
```

```
22:    return (start+end)/2;
23: }
```

If take it serious, there is an efficient way(math) to resolve this problem. Newton iteration algorithm!

```
1:    const float EPS = 0.000000001;
2:    int sqrt(int x) {
3:        // Start typing your C/C++ solution below
4:        // DO NOT write int main() function
5:        if(x==0) return x;
6:        float dividend = x;
7:        float val = x;//final
8:        float last;//previous value
9:        do
10:       {
11:           last = val;
12:           val =(val + dividend/val) / 2;
13:       }while(abs(val-last) > EPS);
14:       int result = val;
15:       if(result * result > x)
16:           result--;
17:       return result;
18:   }
```

[Note]
For the Newton iteration solution, Line 15 & 16 will handle the iterating overflow. E.g., if x is 2147395599,the result will be 46340, not 46339.

112. String to Integer (atoi)

Implement atoi to convert a string to an integer.

Hint: Carefully consider all possible input cases. If you want a challenge, please do not see below and ask yourself what are the possible input cases.

Notes: It is intended for this problem to be specified vaguely (ie, no given input specs). You are responsible to gather all the input requirements up front.

Requirements for atoi:

The function first discards as many whitespace characters as necessary until the first non-whitespace character is found.

Then, starting from this character, takes an optional initial plus or minus sign followed by as many numerical digits as possible, and interprets them as a numerical value.

The string can contain additional characters after those that form the integral number, which are ignored and have no effect on the behavior of this function.

If the first sequence of non-whitespace characters in str is not a valid integral number, or if no such sequence exists because either str is empty or it contains only whitespace characters, no conversion is performed.

If no valid conversion could be performed, a zero value is returned. If the correct value is out of the range of representable values, INT_MAX (2147483647) or INT_MIN (-2147483648) is returned.

» Solve this problem

[Thoughts]

No algrithom here, but really test your Carefulness. Need good implementation and careful thoughts. Pay attention to several special cases, like:

1. irregular format.
   "-3924x8fc", " + 413",
2. invalid input
   " ++c", " ++1"
3. overflow
   "2147483648"

[Code]

```
1:  int atoi(const char *str) {
2:      int num=0;
3:      int sign =1;
4:      int len = strlen(str);
5:      int i =0;
6:      while(str[i] == ' ' && i< len) i++;
7:      if(str[i] == '+') i++;
8:      if(str[i] == '-')
9:      {
10:         sign = -1;
11:         i++;
12:     }
13:     for(;i<len; i++)
14:     {
15:         if(str[i] == ' ') break;
16:         if(str[i]<'0' || str[i] > '9') break;
17:         if(INT_MAX/10 < num
18:             || INT_MAX/10 == num
19:             && INT_MAX%10 < (str[i] -'0'))
20:         {
21:             return sign == -1 ? INT_MIN : INT_MAX;
22:             break;
23:         }
24:         num = num*10 + str[i] -'0';
25:     }
26:     return num*sign;
27: }
```

113. Subsets

Given a set of distinct integers, *S*, return all possible subsets.
Note:

- Elements in a subset must be in non-descending order.
- The solution set must not contain duplicate subsets.

For example,
If *S* = [1,2,3], a solution is:

```
[
  [3],
  [1],
  [2],
  [1,2,3],
  [1,3],
  [2,3],
  [1,2],
  []
]
```

» Solve this problem

[Thoughts]
A classic combination. We can solve it by recursion. The logic is:

Func GenerateSet
    For each number N in S
        Push N into subset and print
        If N is not the last number in S
            Execute GenerateSet on next num recursively.

[Code]
```
1:  vector<vector<int> > subsets(vector<int> &S) {
2:      vector<vector<int> > result;
3:      vector<int> output;
4:      if(S.size() ==0) return result;
5:      result.push_back(output); // the empty set
6:      sort(S.begin(), S.end());
```

```
7:       generateSub(S, 0, result, output);
8: }
9: void generateSub(
10:      vector<int> &s,
11:      int step,
12:      vector<vector<int> > &result,
13:      vector<int>& output)
14: {
15:      for(int i = step;i<s.size(); i++ )
16:      {
17:         output.push_back(s[i]);
18:         result.push_back(output);
19:         if(i< s.size()-1)
20:             generateSub(s, i+1, result, output);
21:         output.pop_back();
22:      }
23: }
```

114. Subsets II

Given a collection of integers that might contain duplicates, *S*, return all possible subsets.

Note:

- Elements in a subset must be in non-descending order.
- The solution set must not contain duplicate subsets.

For example,

If *S* = [1,2,2], a solution is:

```
[
    [2],
    [1],
    [1,2,2],
    [2,2],
    [1,2],
    []
]
```

» Solve this problem

[Thoughts]
Like previous one. The difference is about how to remove the duplicate. Line 24, 25 is the magic code to filter the duplicate number. If the next number is same as current(duplicate), filter it.

[Code]
```
1:  vector<vector<int> > subsetsWithDup(vector<int> &S) {
2:      vector<vector<int> > result;
3:      vector<int> output;
4:      if(S.size() ==0) return result;
5:      result.push_back(output);
6:      sort(S.begin(), S.end());
7:      generateSub(S, 0, result, output);
8:  }
9:
```

```
10:  void generateSub(
11:      vector<int> &s,
12:      int step,
13:      vector<vector<int> > &result,
14:      vector<int>& output)
15:  {
16:      for(int i = step;i<s.size(); i++ )
17:      {
18:          output.push_back(s[i]);
19:          result.push_back(output);
20:          if(i< s.size()-1)
21:              generateSub(s, i+1, result, output);
22:          output.pop_back();
23:          while(i<s.size()-1 && s[i] == s[i+1])
24:              i++;
25:      }
26:  }
27:
```

115. Substring with Concatenation of All Words

You are given a string, **S**, and a list of words, **L**, that are all of the same length. Find all starting indices of substring(s) in S that is a concatenation of each word in L exactly once and without any intervening characters.
For example, given:
S: "barfoothefoobarman"
L: ["foo", "bar"]
You should return the indices: [0,9].
(order does not matter).
» Solve this problem

[Thoughts]
No pretty solution. Use two maps to track the appearance of the word in L. Scan S from left to right.

[Code]
```
1:  vector<int> findSubstring(string S, vector<string> &L) {
2:      map<string, int> expectCount;
3:      map<string, int> realCount;
4:      for(int i =0; i< L.size(); i++)
5:      {
6:          expectCount[L.at(i)]++;
7:      }
8:      vector<int> result;
9:      int row = L.size();
10:     if(row ==0) return result;
11:     int len = L[0].size();
12:     for(int i =0; i< (int)S.size() - row*len+1; i++)
13:     {
14:         realCount.clear();
15:         int j =0;
16:         for(; j< row; j++)
```

```
17:        {
18:            string sub = S.substr(i+j*len, len);
19:            if(expectCount.find(sub) != expectCount.end())
20:            {
21:                realCount[sub]++;
22:            }
23:            else
24:                break;
25:            if(realCount[sub] > expectCount[sub])
26:            {
27:                break;
28:            }
29:        }
30:        if(j == row)
31:            result.push_back(i);
32:    }
33:    return result;
34: }
```

[Note]
A tricky in Line 14 as highlight in red. The type of S.size() is unsigned int, if not convert to int, the result will be promoted to unsigned int. For example, (unsigned int) 1 - (int)2, the final result is not -1, but 4294967295.

116. Sum Root to Leaf Numbers

Given a binary tree containing digits from 0-9 only, each root-to-leaf path could represent a number.
An example is the root-to-leaf path 1->2->3 which represents the number 123.
Find the total sum of all root-to-leaf numbers.
For example,

```
    1
   / \
  2   3
```

The root-to-leaf path 1->2 represents the number 12.
The root-to-leaf path 1->3 represents the number 13.
Return the sum = 12 + 13 = 25.
» Solve this problem

[Thoughts]
This is similar problem as prior "Binary Tree Maximum Path Sum".
the difference here is only adding a track variable to sum all the paths.

[Code]

```
1: int sumNumbers(TreeNode *root) {
2:     int sum=0, path =0;
3:     GenerateSum(root, sum, path);
4:     return sum;
5: }
6: void GenerateSum(TreeNode *root, int& sum, int path)
7: {
8:     if(root == NULL) return;
9:     path = path*10 +root->val;
10:    if(root->left == NULL && root->right == NULL)
11:    {
12:        sum+=path;
```

```
13:        return;
14:    }
15:    GenerateSum(root->left, sum, path);
16:    GenerateSum(root->right, sum, path);
17: }
```

117. Surrounded Regions

Given a 2D board containing 'X' and 'O', capture all regions surrounded by 'X'.
A region is captured by flipping all 'O's into 'X's in that surrounded region .
For example,

```
X X X X

X O O X

X X O X

X O X X
```

After running your function, the board should be:

```
X X X X

X X X X

X X X X

X O X X
```

» Solve this problem

[Thoughts]
We can do the BFS for radom O, and keeping tracking all the nearby cells until no O around. Then, clean the region if no O is in the boundary. But this will cost lots of memory if this is a big board since for each O, you need to maintain a snapshot of the region.

Do we need to pick up the O randomly? No, the problem already says the region will only be cleaned if no O is in boundary. Let's take advantage of this constraint.
1. Pick the O in the boundary and start the search. All the region will be marked by a new symbol, like Y.
2. Scan the whole board. For each cell,
    a. If the cell is O, it means it belongs to a region which has no O in the boundary. Definitely, we need to clean it and change its value to X.

b. If the cell is Y, it means this cell belongs to a region which shouldn't be cleaned. So, revert its value back from Y to O.
c. If the cell is X. Skip.

[Code]

```
1:  vector<int> xIndex;
2:  vector<int> yIndex;
3:  void solve(vector<vector<char>> &board) {
4:      int row = board.size();
5:      if(row == 0) return;
6:      int col = board[0].size();
7:      xIndex.clear();
8:      yIndex.clear();
9:      for(int i =0; i< row; i++)
10:     {
11:         if(board[i][0] == 'O') {
12:             xIndex.push_back(i);
13:             yIndex.push_back(0);
14:         }
15:         if(board[i][col-1] == 'O') {
16:             xIndex.push_back(i);
17:             yIndex.push_back(col-1);
18:         }
19:     }
20:     for(int i =0; i< col; i++)
21:     {
22:         if(board[0][i] == 'O') {
23:             xIndex.push_back(0);
24:             yIndex.push_back(i);
25:         }
26:         if(board[row-1][i] == 'O') {
27:             xIndex.push_back(row-1);
28:             yIndex.push_back(i);
29:         }
```

```
30:    }
31:    int k =0;
32:    while(k<xIndex.size())
33:    {
34:        int x = xIndex[k];
35:        int y = yIndex[k];
36:        board[x][y] = 'Y';
37:        if(x>0 && board[x-1][y] == 'O' ) {
38:            xIndex.push_back(x-1);
39:            yIndex.push_back(y);
40:        }
41:        if(x<row-1 && board[x+1][y] == 'O') {
42:            xIndex.push_back(x+1);
43:            yIndex.push_back(y);
44:        }
45:        if(y>0 && board[x][y-1] == 'O' ) {
46:            xIndex.push_back(x);
47:            yIndex.push_back(y-1);
48:        }
49:        if(y<col-1 && board[x][y+1] == 'O' ) {
50:            xIndex.push_back(x);
51:            yIndex.push_back(y+1);
52:        }
53:        k++;
54:    }
55:    for(int i =0; i< row; i++)
56:    {
57:        for(int j =0; j< col; j++)
58:        {
59:            if(board[i][j] =='O') board[i][j] = 'X';
60:            if(board[i][j] == 'Y') board[i][j] = 'O';
61:        }
62:    }
63: }
```

118. Swap Nodes in Pairs

Given a linked list, swap every two adjacent nodes and return its head.
For example,
Given 1->2->3->4, you should return the list as 2->1->4->3.
Your algorithm should use only constant space. You may **not** modify the values in the list, only nodes itself can be changed.
» Solve this problem

[Thoughts]
Two-pointers switch. Need to think about some special condition, like empty list, only 1 item in a list, only two items in a list. And also think about the head node will also be changed during switching.
Adding a safeguard can make the logic much simpler.

[Code]
```
1:  ListNode *swapPairs(ListNode *head) {
2:     if(head == NULL) return NULL;
3:     if(head->next == NULL) return head;
4:     ListNode* safeG = new ListNode(-1);
5:     safeG->next= head; // head will be changed in next switch
6:     ListNode *pre = head->next;
7:     ListNode *cur = head;
8:     ListNode *post = safeG;
9:     while(pre!=NULL)
10:    {
11:        ListNode* temp = pre->next;
12:        pre->next = cur;
13:        cur->next = temp;
14:        post->next = pre;
15:        post= cur;
16:        if(post->next == NULL) break;
17:        cur = post->next;
18:        pre = cur->next;
```

```
19:    }
20:        head = safeG->next;
21:        delete safeG;
22:        return head;
23: }
```

Recursion(more concise)

```
1:    ListNode *swapPairs(ListNode *head) {
2:        if (head == NULL || head->next == NULL) {
3:            return head;
4:        }
5:        ListNode* nextPair = head->next->next;
6:        ListNode* newHead = head->next;
7:        head->next->next = head;
8:        head->next = swapPairs(nextPair);
9:        return newHead;
10:   }
```

119. Symmetric Tree

Given a binary tree, check whether it is a mirror of itself (ie, symmetric around its center).

For example, this binary tree is symmetric:

```
        1
       / \
      2   2
     / \ / \
    3  4 4  3
```

But the following is not:

```
        1
       / \
      2   2
       \   \
       3   3
```

Note:

Bonus points if you could solve it both recursively and iteratively.

confused what `"{1,#,2,3}"` means? > read more on how binary tree is serialized on OJ.

» Solve this problem

[Thoughts]

Two ways to solve this problem:

1. Iteration. Travel the tree by level and check the symmetric in each level.
2. Recursion. For each tree node, it is symmetric if
   a. Left node equals right node, or they are both null
   b. The left sub-tree of left node is symmetric with the right sub-tree of right node
   c. The right sub-tree of left node is symmetric with the left sub-tree of right node

[Code]

Iteration:

```
1:  bool isSymmetric(TreeNode *root) {
```

```
2:      if(root == NULL) return true;
3:      vector<TreeNode*> visitQueue;
4:      visitQueue.push_back(root);
5:      int curLevel=1;
6:      while(curLevel >0)
7:      {
8:        int i=0;
9:        while(i<curLevel)
10:       {
11:           TreeNode* p = visitQueue[i];
12:           i++;
13:           if(p==NULL) continue;
14:           visitQueue.push_back(p->left);
15:           visitQueue.push_back(p->right);
16:       }
17:       int start = 0, end = curLevel-1;
18:       while(start< end)
19:       {
20:           TreeNode *pl = visitQueue[start];
21:           TreeNode *pr = visitQueue[end];
22:           int l = pl== NULL? -1:pl->val;
23:           int r = pr== NULL? -1: pr->val;
24:           if(l!=r)
25:               return false;
26:           start++;
27:           end--;
28:       }
29:       visitQueue.erase(visitQueue.begin(), visitQueue.begin() + curLevel);
30:       curLevel = visitQueue.size();
31:     }
32:     return true;
33: }
```

Recursion:

```
1:  bool isSymmetric(TreeNode *root) {
2:      if(root == NULL) return true;
3:      return isSym(root->left, root->right);
4:  }
5:  bool isSym(TreeNode *left, TreeNode *right)
6:  {
7:      if(left == NULL)
8:          return right ==NULL;
9:      if(right == NULL)
10:         return left == NULL;
11:     if(left->val != right->val)
12:         return false;
13:     if(!isSym(left->left, right->right))
14:         return false;
15:     if(!isSym(left->right, right->left))
16:         return false;
17:     return true;
18: }
```

120. Text Justification

Given an array of words and a length *L*, format the text such that each line has exactly *L* characters and is fully (left and right) justified.

You should pack your words in a greedy approach; that is, pack as many words as you can in each line. Pad extra spaces' ' when necessary so that each line has exactly *L* characters.

Extra spaces between words should be distributed as evenly as possible. If the number of spaces on a line do not divide evenly between words, the empty slots on the left will be assigned more spaces than the slots on the right.

For the last line of text, it should be left justified and no extra space is inserted between words.

For example,

words: ["This", "is", "an", "example", "of", "text", "justification."]
L: 16.
Return the formatted lines as:

```
[
   "This    is    an",
   "example  of text",
   "justification.   "
]
```

Note: Each word is guaranteed not to exceed *L* in length.
Corner Cases:
  • A line other than the last line might contain only one word. What should you do in this case?
  In this case, that line should be left-justified.

» Solve this problem

[Thoughts]
A trivial implementation problem. Writing the whole function only spends less than 20 minutes, but it will cost one hour to debug and make it pass.

[Code]
```
1:  vector<string> fullJustify(vector<string> &words, int L) {
```

```
2:      vector<string> result;
3:      if(0 == words.size()) return result;
4:      int i =0;
5:      while(i< words.size())
6:      {
7:          int start = i;
8:          int sum = 0;
9:          while(i<words.size() && sum + words[i].size()<=L)
10:         {
11:             sum+=words[i].size() +1;
12:             i++;
13:         }
14:         int end = i-1;
15:         int intervalCount = end - start;
16:         int avgSp = 0, leftSp = 0;
17:         if(intervalCount >0)
18:         {
19:             avgSp = (L-sum + intervalCount+1)/intervalCount;
20:             leftSp = (L-sum + intervalCount+1)%intervalCount;
21:         }
22:         string line;
23:         for(int j = start; j<end; j++)
24:         {
25:             line+=words[j];
26:             if(i == words.size()) // the last line
27:                 line.append(1,' ');
28:             else
29:             {
30:                 line.append(avgSp,' '); //average space
31:                 if(leftSp>0) // the extra space
32:                 {
33:                     line.append(1,' ');
34:                     leftSp--;
35:                 }
36:             }
```

```
37:        }
38:        line+=words[end];
39:        if(line.size()<L)
40:            line.append(L-line.size(), ' ');
41:        result.push_back(line);
42:    }
43:    return result;
44: }
```

121. Trapping Rain Water

Given *n* non-negative integers representing an elevation map
where the width of each bar is 1, compute how much water it is
able to trap after raining.
For example,
Given [0,1,0,2,1,0,1,3,2,1,2,1], return 6.

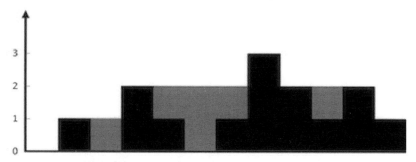

The above elevation map is represented by array
[0,1,0,2,1,0,1,3,2,1,2,1]. In this case, 6 units of rain water (blue section)
are being trapped.**Thanks Marcos** for contributing this image!
» Solve this problem

[Thoughts]
Look at each bar, its capacity of holding water is depending on
the height difference between the max left and the max right. So,
if we define H[i] as the max units water this bar can hold, easy to
get following equation:

$$H[i] = min(\ Max(\ Array[j]\ ),\ Max(\ Array[k])\ ) - Array[i] \quad where \\ j<i\ and\ k>i$$

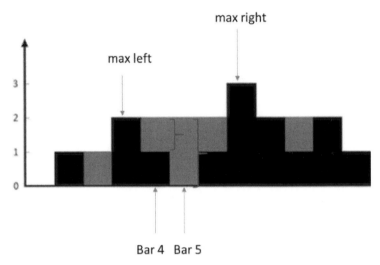

Bar 4   Bar 5

For example, Bar 4 and Bar 5 has the same max left and max right. The red brackets show that how the water size is calculated.

Algrithom is simple here, for each bar
1. Scan from let to right, and get the MaxLeft for each bar
2. Scan from right to left, and get the MaxRight for each bar
3. Scan from left to right again, apply the calculation equation for each bar, and sum the water size

[Code]

In the implementation, iteration #2 and iteration #3 can be processed in one round scan.

```
1:  int trap(int A[], int n) {
2:     if(n<2) return 0;
3:     int *maxL = new int[n], *maxR=new int[n];
4:     int max = A[0];
5:     maxL[0] =0;
6:     for(int i =1; i<n-1; i++)
7:     {
8:        maxL[i] =max;
9:        if(max < A[i])
10:            max = A[i];
11:    }
```

```
12:    max=A[n-1];
13:    maxR[n-1]=0;
14:    int ctrap,ttrap=0;
15:    for(int i = n-2; i>0; i--)
16:    {
17:        maxR[i] = max;
18:        ctrap = min(maxL[i], maxR[i]) -A[i];
19:        if(ctrap>0)
20:            ttrap+=ctrap;
21:        if(max<A[i])
22:            max = A[i];
23:    }
24:    delete maxL, maxR;
25:    return ttrap;
26: }
```

Note:
This problem can be transformed to a little challenge. If not ask for the whole volume, but ask for the max volumn. How do you plan to resolve this?

122. Triangle

Given a triangle, find the minimum path sum from top to bottom.
Each step you may move to adjacent numbers on the row below.
For example, given the following triangle

```
[
     [2],
    [3,4],
   [6,5,7],
  [4,1,8,3]
]
```

The minimum path sum from top to bottom
is 11 (i.e., 2 + 3 + 5 + 1 = 11).
Note:
Bonus point if you are able to do this using only O(n) extra
space, where n is the total number of rows in the triangle.
» Solve this problem

[Thoughts]
One dimension dynamic programming. Actually, this problem is
easy to calculate from bottom to up. Otherwise, you need to pay
more attention to the handle the index boundary and the initia
value.

Define MinV[i][j] as the minimal path sum at (i,j). And the
equation will like following:

$$MinV[i][j] = array[i][j] \quad if\ i == row\text{-}1$$
$$Or$$
$$= min(\ MinV[i+1][j],\ MinV[i+1][j+1]\ ) + array[i][j] \quad if\ i != row\text{-}1$$

[Code]
```
1:  int minimumTotal(vector<vector<int> > &triangle) {
2:    int row = triangle.size();
3:    if(row ==0) return 0;
4:    vector<int> minV(triangle[row-1].size());
5:    for(int i =row-1; i>=0; i--)
```

```
6:    {
7:        int col = triangle[i].size();
8:        for(int j =0; j<col; j++)
9:        {
10:           if(i == row-1)
11:           {
12:               minV[j] = triangle[i][j];
13:               continue;
14:           }
15:           minV[j] = min(minV[j], minV[j+1]) + triangle[i][j];
16:        }
17:    }
18:    return minV[0];
19: }
```

123. Unique Binary Search Trees

Given *n*, how many structurally unique **BST's** (binary search trees) that store values 1...*n*?
For example,
Given *n* = 3, there are a total of 5 unique BST's.

```
    1           3       3       2         1
     \         /       /       / \         \
      3       2       1       1   3         2
     /       /         \                     \
    2       1           2                     3
```

» Solve this problem

[Thoughts]
If you look at the example in the problem description, it might take you quite long to figure out the internal pattern of data. But if we change the sequence a little bit as below, it will be much easier to find it out,

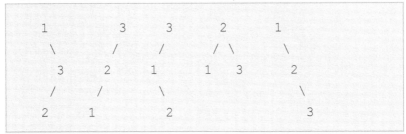

For example, if we choose [1] as the root node, how many unique BST it can generate really depends on how many sub unique BST the left two nodes[2,3] could generate. And if we choose [2] as the root node, the number of unique BST really relys on how many unique BST one node can generate(one node for left, one for right). In the end, if we choose [3] as the root node, it will be same as choosing [1] as the root,

Suppose the input array is S. If defines Count[i] as the unique BST number generated by nodes [0,i], we can easily infer that:

If S = ∅, no doubt, there is only one BST, the empty tree.
So
    Count[0] =1

if S= {1}, there is still only one BST, the single node tree.
So
    Count[1] = 1

If S ={1,2}, there will be two unique BST as below:

```
1                2
 \              /
  2            1
```

So,
    Count[2] =   Count[0] * Count[1]   (1 is the root)
                + Count[1] * Count[0]   (2 is the root)

If S = {1,2,3}, same as the example in the problem description, we can get the unique BST could be calculated as
    Count[3] =   Count[0]*Count[2] (1 is the root)
                + Count[1]*Count[1] (2 is the root)
                + Count[2]*Count[0] (3 is the root)

Till now, we can theoretically infer the generic recurrence formula:

```
Count[i]  = ∑ Count[0...k]  * Count[
k+1....i]      0<=k<i-1
```

[Code]

```
1:  int numTrees(int n) {
2:     vector<int> count(n+1, 0);
3:     count[0] =1;
4:     count[1] =1;
5:     for(int i =2; i<=n; i++)
6:     {
7:         for(int j =0; j<i; j++)
8:         {
```

```
9:              count[i] += count[j]*count[i-j-1];
10:        }
11:    }
12:    return count[n];
13: }
```

[Note]

This is an interesting problem. For most people, the thing blocking their thought is how to judge whether a BST is unique or not. There is one theorem for defining the unique BST.

> *Define an array as [1,2,3,4, … i, …, n]. The BST is unique if the tree is built with i as the root, and its left sub-tree is built by [0, i-1] and its right sub-tree is built by [i+1, n].*

124. Unique Binary Search Trees II

Given *n*, generate all structurally unique **BST's** (binary search trees) that store values 1...*n*.
For example,
Given *n* = 3, your program should return all 5 unique BST's shown below.

```
    1           3       3       2         1
     \         /       /       / \         \
      3       2       1       1   3         2
     /       /         \                     \
    2       1           2                     3
```

confused what "{1,#,2,3}" means? > read more on how binary tree is serialized on OJ.
» Solve this problem

[Thoughts]
The idea is same as previous "Unique Binary Search Trees". The difference is this problem needs to outpu all the BST instances.

The solution is same. Choose a root node and build the left sub-tree and right sub-tree recursively.

[Code]

```
1:  vector<TreeNode *> generateTrees(int n) {
2:    if(n ==0) return *generate(1,0);
3:    return *generate(1, n);
4:  }
5:  vector<TreeNode *>* generate(int start, int end)
6:  {
7:    vector<TreeNode *> *subTree =
8:              new vector<TreeNode*>();
```

```
9:    if(start>end)
10:   {
11:       subTree->push_back(NULL);
12:       return subTree;
13:   }
14:   for(int i =start; i<=end; i++)
15:   {
16:       vector<TreeNode*> *leftSubs =
17:                     generate(start, i-1);
18:       vector<TreeNode*> *rightSubs =
19:                     generate(i+1, end);
20:       for(int j = 0; j< leftSubs->size(); j++)
21:       {
22:          for(int k=0; k<rightSubs->size(); k++)
23:          {
24:              TreeNode *node = new TreeNode(i);
25:              node->left = (*leftSubs)[j];
26:              node->right = (*rightSubs)[k];
27:              subTree->push_back(node);
28:          }
29:       }
30:   }
31:   return subTree;
32: }
```

125. Unique Paths

A robot is located at the top-left corner of a *m* x *n* grid (marked
'Start' in the diagram below).
The robot can only move either down or right at any point in time.
The robot is trying to reach the bottom-right corner of the grid
(marked 'Finish' in the diagram below).
How many possible unique paths are there?

Above is a 3 x 7 grid. How many possible unique paths are there?
Note: *m* and *n* will be at most 100.
» Solve this problem

[Thoughts]
One dimension dynamic programming.
Definition:
Step[i][j] means the unique paths from (0,0) to (i,j)
And easy to get get Step[i][j] in somewhat more general terms:

```
Step[i][j] = 1          i=0 && j=0
     or
            = Step[i-1][j] + Step[i][j-1]
                  i!=0 || j!=0
```

[Code]
In implementation, we don't really define two-dimensional array.
Use an iterative array.

```
1:    int uniquePaths(int m, int n) {
2:        vector<int> maxV(n,0);
```

```
3:        maxV[0]=1;
4:        for(int i =0; i< m; i++)
5:        {
6:            for(int j =1; j<n; j++)
7:            {
8:                maxV[j] = maxV[j-1] + maxV[j];
9:            }
10:       }
11:       return maxV[n-1];
12:   }
```

126. Unique Paths II

Follow up for "Unique Paths":
Now consider if some obstacles are added to the grids. How many unique paths would there be?
An obstacle and empty space is marked as 1 and 0 respectively in the grid.
For example,
There is one obstacle in the middle of a 3x3 grid as illustrated below.

```
[
  [0,0,0],
  [0,1,0],
  [0,0,0]
]
```

The total number of unique paths is 2.
Note: *m* and *n* will be at most 100.
» Solve this problem

[Thoughts]
Similar as problem 'Unique Path'.
Only one different in the equation(highlight):

$$Step[i][j] = 1 \quad i=0 \text{ \&\& } j=0$$
Or
$$= Step[i-1][j] + Step[i][j-1] \quad \text{if Array}[i][j] ==0$$
Or
$$= 0 \quad \text{if Array}[i][j] =1$$

[Code]
```
1:    int uniquePathsWithObstacles(vector<vector<int> >
&obstacleGrid) {
2:        int m = obstacleGrid.size();
3:        if(m ==0) return 0;
4:        int n = obstacleGrid[0].size();
5:        if(obstacleGrid[0][0] ==1) return 0;
6:        vector<int> maxV(n,0);
```

```
7:      maxV[0] =1;
8:      for(int i =0; i<m; i++)
9:      {
10:         for(int j =0; j<n; j++)
11:         {
12:            if(obstacleGrid[i][j] ==1)
13:               maxV[j]=0;
14:            else if(j >0)
15:               maxV[j] = maxV[j-1]+maxV[j];
16:         }
17:      }
18:      return maxV[n-1];
19:   }
```

127. Upcase and lowcase permutation

Give a string, which only contains a-z. List all the permutation of upcase and lowcase.
For example, str = "ab", the output should be
"ab", "aB", "Ab", "AB"
for str = "abc", the output should be
"abc", "abC", "aBc", "aBC", "Abc", "AbC", "ABc", "ABC"

[Thoughts]
It is pretty sure that this problem could be solved by recursion. Since each character has only two status: Upcase or Lowcase, the code could be written simply as below.

```
1:  void ListPermutation(string sample, int depth, string& result)
2:  {
3:      if(depth == sample.size())
4:      {
5:          prinf("%s\r\n", result.c_str());
6:          return;
7:      }
8:      // process low-case char
9:      result.push_back(sample[depth]);
10:     ListPermutation(sample, depth+1, result);
11:     result.pop_back();
12:     //process up-case char
13:     result.push_back(sample[depth]-32);
14:     ListPermutation(sample, depth+1, result);
15:     result.pop_back();
16: }
```

The code is brief. But if we think about the complexity of memory, this solution doesn't sound feasible, expecially when the input string has tens of thousands charators.
Let's change another way to target this problem. As the problem described, each charator has only two states: Up or Low. We

can use binary to define it : 1 means Upcase and 0 means Lowcae. If the length of the input string is L, then, we only need to iteration each integer between [0, 2^L-1]. For every integer i, convert it to the binary format string with L length, and then, decide the upcase or lowcase based on the value in each bit. In this solution, the complexity of memory will be only O(L).

[Code]

```
1:  void ListPermutation(string sample)
2:  {
3:      int L = sample.size();
4:      long end = pow(2, L) -1;
5:      for(int i =0; i< end; i++)
6:      {
7:          // Convert Dec to Binary,
8:          // return a string to represent binary data with size L
9:          string binaryRep = ConvertDecToBinany(i, L);
10:         string output;
11:         for(int j=0; j<L; j++)
12:         {
13:             if(binaryRep[j] == '0') //low case
14:             {
15:                 output.push_back(sample[j]);
16:             }
17:             else
18:             {
19:                 output.push_back(sample[j]-32);
20:             }
21:         }
22:         printf("%s\r\n", output.c_str());
23:     }
24: }
```

128. Valid Palindrome

Given a string, determine if it is a palindrome, considering only alphanumeric characters and ignoring cases.
For example,
`"A man, a plan, a canal: Panama"` is a palindrome.
`"race a car"` is *not* a palindrome.
Note:
Have you consider that the string might be empty? This is a good question to ask during an interview.
For the purpose of this problem, we define empty string as valid palindrome.
» Solve this problem

[Thoughts]
This is a classic two-pointer scanning problem. We can use two pointers which points to the head and the tail of the string. And then, do the scan from both sides to middle.

[Code]

```
1:  bool isPalindrome(string s) {
2:      int start = 0;
3:      int end = s.size()-1;
4:      std::transform(
5:          s.begin(), s.end(), s.begin(), ::tolower);
6:      while(start<end)
7:      {
8:          //filter non-alpha char
9:          while(start< end && !isAlpha(s[start])) start++;
10:         //filter non-alpha char
11:         while(start< end && !isAlpha(s[end])) end--;
12:         if(s[start]!=s[end]) break;
13:         start++;
14:         end--;
15:     }
```

```
16:    if(start >= end)
17:        return true;
18:    else
19:        return false;
20: }
21: bool isAlpha(char c)
22: {
23:    if(c>='a' && c<='z') return true;
24:    if(c>='0' && c<='9') return true;
25:    return false;
26: }
```

129. Valid Parentheses

Given a string containing just the
characters '(', ')', '{', '}', '[' and ']', determine if the
input string is valid.
The brackets must close in the correct
order, "()" and "()[]{}" are all valid but "(]" and "([)]" are
not.
» Solve this problem

[Thoughts]
A classic parentheses match via stack. Given one stack, push
the left bracket, and pop it when meet a right bracket. Check
whether the stack is empty at the end.

[Code]
```
1:  bool isValid(string s) {
2:      vector<char> sta;
3:      if(s.size() ==0) return false;
4:      sta.push_back(s[0]);
5:      for(int i =1; i< s.size(); i++)
6:      {
7:          if(s[i] == '(' || s[i] == '[' || s[i] == '{')
8:          {
9:              sta.push_back(s[i]);
10:             continue;
11:         }
12:         char current = sta.back();
13:         if(s[i] == ')' && current != '(') return false;
14:         if(s[i] == ']' && current != '[') return false;
15:         if(s[i] == '}' && current != '{') return false;
16:         sta.pop_back();
17:     }
18:     if(sta.size() !=0) return false;
19:     return true;
20: }
```

130. Valid Sudoku

Determine if a Sudoku is valid, according to: Sudoku Puzzles - The Rules.
The Sudoku board could be partially filled, where empty cells are filled with the character ' . '.

5	3			7				
6			1	9	5			
	9	8					6	
8				6				3
4			8		3			1
7				2				6
	6					2	8	
			4	1	9			5
				8			7	9

A partially filled sudoku which is valid.
» Solve this problem

[Thoughts]
Just an implementation.
1. Check each row
2. Check each column
3. Check the sub-squares(9 cells)

[Code]
```
1:  bool isValidSudoku(vector<vector<char> > &board) {
2:      if(board.size() == 0) return false;
3:      int row[9], col[9];
4:      for(int i =0; i<9; i++)
5:      {
6:          memset(row, 0, 9*sizeof(int));
7:          memset(col, 0, 9*sizeof(int));
```

```
8:         for(int j =0; j<9; j++)
9:         {
10:            if(board[i][j] != '.')
11:            {
12:                if(row[board[i][j]-49] ==1)
13:                    return false;
14:                row[board[i][j]-49]++;
15:            }
16:            if(board[j][i] != '.')
17:            {
18:                if(col[board[j][i]-49] ==1)
19:                    return false;
20:                col[board[j][i]-49]++;
21:            }
22:         }
23:     }
24:     for(int i =0; i< 9; i+=3)
25:     {
26:         for(int j =0; j<9; j+=3)
27:         {
28:             memset(row, 0, 9*sizeof(int));
29:             for(int m=0; m<3; m++)
30:             {
31:                 for(int n =0; n<3; n++)
32:                 {
33:                     if(board[m+i][n+j] == '.')
34:                         continue;
35:                     if(row[board[m+i][n+j]-49] ==1)
36:                         return false;
37:                     row[board[m+i][n+j]-49]++;
38:                 }
39:             }
40:         }
41:     }
42:     return true;
```

```
43: }
44:
```

[Note]
If extend this problem to "Generate a valid Sudoku", how you plan to solve it?

131. Validate Binary Search Tree

Given a binary tree, determine if it is a valid binary search tree (BST).
Assume a BST is defined as follows:
- The left subtree of a node contains only nodes with keys **less than** the node's key.
- The right subtree of a node contains only nodes with keys **greater than** the node's key.
- Both the left and right subtrees must also be binary search trees.

confused what `"{1,#,2,3}"` means?

» Solve this problem

[Thoughts]
Recursion. For every tree node, check whether the left sub-tree is less than root, and the right sub-tree is larger than root.

Another solution is, travel this tree in-order and check whether the travel path is increasing!

[Code]
```
1:    bool isValidBST(TreeNode *root) {
2:        return IsValidBST(root, INT_MIN, INT_MAX);
3:    }
4:    bool IsValidBST(TreeNode* node, int MIN, int MAX)
5:    {
6:        if(node == NULL)
7:            return true;
8:        if(node->val > MIN
9:                && node->val < MAX
10:                && IsValidBST(node->left,MIN,node->val)
11:                && IsValidBST(node->right,node->val,MAX))
12:            return true;
13:        else
14:            return false;
15:    }
```

132. Wildcard Matching

Implement wildcard pattern matching with support
for '?' and '*'.

```
'?' Matches any single character.
'*' Matches any sequence of characters
(including the empty sequence).

The matching should cover the entire input
string (not partial).

The function prototype should be:
bool isMatch(const char *s, const char *p)

Some examples:
isMatch("aa","a") → false
isMatch("aa","aa") → true
isMatch("aaa","aa") → false
isMatch("aa", "*") → true
isMatch("aa", "a*") → true
isMatch("ab", "?*") → true
isMatch("aab", "c*a*b") → false
```

» Solve this problem

[Thoughts]
String match, the tricky part is how to match *. If p meets a *,
store the index of * and also s. Then, s continues to match the
left p, if match fails, revert s and p to previous stored index. And
continue the search with the next char(s++).

[Code]
```
1:  bool isMatch(const char *s, const char *p) {
2:      bool star = false;
3:      const char *str, *ptr;
4:      for(str = s, ptr =p; *str!='\0'; str++, ptr++)
5:      {
6:          switch(*ptr)
```

```
7:      {
8:          case '?':
9:              break;
10:         case '*':
11:             star =true;
12:             s=str, p =ptr;
13:             while(*p=='*')
14:                 p++;
15:             if(*p == '\0') // if nil after '*', return true
16:                 return true;
17:             str = s-1;
18:             ptr = p-1;
19:             break;
20:         default:
21:             {
22:                 if(*str != *ptr)
23:                 {
24:                     // if no '*' in front, match failed
25:                     if(!star)
26:                         return false;
27:                     s++;
28:                     str = s-1;
29:                     ptr = p-1;
30:                 }
31:             }
32:         }
33:     }
34:     while(*ptr== '*')
35:         ptr++;
36:     return (*ptr == '\0');
37: }
```

133. Word Break

Given a string *s* and a dictionary of words *dict*, determine if *s* can be segmented into a space-separated sequence of one or more dictionary words.

For example, given
s = `"leetcode"`,
dict = `["leet", "code"]`.

Return true because `"leetcode"` can be segmented as `"leet code"`.

[Thoughts]
This is a DP problem. Let's use some notations to defind this problem first.

Definition

```
S : the input string
possible[i] : represents whether S[0,i] can
be segmented by dictionary.
```

With these notations, we can redefine the proble as below

possible[i]
   = true   if S[0,i] can be segmented
   = true   if there exist a k(0<k<i), which makes

         possible[k] == true **and** S[k+1,j] is in the dictionary
   = false if   no such k exist.

[Code]
In the implementation, add a dummy node in the string (Line2) to simplify the code. If you don't understand why, try to implement one without dummy node and then you will realize the value of dummy node here.

```
1:  bool wordBreak(string s, unordered_set<string> &dict) {
2:      string s2 = '#' + s;
```

```
3:    int len = s2.size();
4:    vector<bool> possible(len, 0);
5:    possible[0] = true;
6:    for(int i =1; i< len; ++i)
7:    {
8:        for(int k=0; k<i; ++k)
9:        {
10:           possible[i] =
11:               possible[k] &&
12:               dict.find(s2.substr(k+1, i-k)) != dict.end();
13:           if(possible[i]) break;
14:        }
15:    }
16:    return possible[len-1];
17: }
```

134. WordBreak II

Given a string *s* and a dictionary of words *dict*, add spaces in *s* to construct a sentence where each word is a valid dictionary word.

Return all such possible sentences.

For example, given
s = "catsanddog",
dict = ["cat", "cats", "and", "sand", "dog"].

A solution is ["cats and dog", "cat sand dog"].

[Thoughts]
It could be solved by DP + memorization. And we can also solve it via recursion + pruning.

Add an array – possible[] to record the possibility of sub-strings.

```
Possible[i] = true means S[i,n] could be
segmented.
```

[Code]
```
1: vector<string> wordBreak(string s, unordered_set<string> &dict) {
2:     string result;
3:     vector<string> solutions;
4:     int len = s.size();
5:     vector<bool> possible(len+1, true);
6:     GetAllSolution(0, s, dict, len, result, solutions, possible);
7:     return solutions;
8: }
9: void GetAllSolution(int start, const string& s,
10:     const unordered_set<string> &dict, int len,
11:     string& result, vector<string>& solutions,
12:     vector<bool>& possible)
13: {
14:     if (start == len)
```

```
15:    {
16:        solutions.push_back(result.substr(0, result.size()-1));
17:        return;
18:    }
19:    for (int i = start; i< len; ++i)
20:    {
21:        string piece = s.substr(start, i - start + 1);
22:        if (dict.find(piece) != dict.end()
23:            && possible[i+1]) // skip unnecessary search
24:        {
25:            result.append(piece).append(" ");
26:            int beforeChange = solutions.size();
27:            GetAllSolution(i + 1, s, dict, len, result, solutions, possible);
28:            if(solutions.size() == beforeChange)
29:            {
30:                // if no solution found, set the possibility to false
31:                possible[i+1] = false;
32:            }
33:            result.resize(result.size() - piece.size()-1);
34:        }
35:    }
36: }
```

135. Word Search

Given a 2D board and a word, find if the word exists in the grid. The word can be constructed from letters of sequentially adjacent cell, where "adjacent" cells are those horizontally or vertically neighboring. The same letter cell may not be used more than once.
For example,
Given **board** =

```
[
    ["ABCE"],
    ["SFCS"],
    ["ADEE"]
]
```

word = "ABCCED", -> returns true,
word = "SEE", -> returns true,
word = "ABCB", -> returns false.

[Thoughts]
Similar as "Unique Paths" problem. The difference here is, previous robat can only go down or right, but here the search can also go up and left, four directions. In case of repeat visiting the same path(especially in a cycle), introduce a new array 'visited' track the path.

[Code]
```
1:  bool exist(vector<vector<char> > &board, string word) {
2:      if(word.size() ==0) return false;
3:      if(board.size() ==0 || board[0].size() == 0) return false;
4:      int row = board.size();
5:      int col = board[0].size();
6:      int * visited = new int[row*col];
7:      memset(visited, 0, row*col*sizeof(int));
8:      for(int i =0; i< board.size(); i++)
9:      {
10:         for(int j =0; j< board[0].size(); j++)
```

```
11:        {
12:            if(board[i][j] == word[0])
13:            {
14:                visited[i*col+j] = 1;
15:                if(search(board, word, visited, -1, 1, i, j))
16:                    return true;
17:                visited[i*col+j] =0;
18:            }
19:        }
20:    }
21:    delete visited;
22:    return false;
23: }
24:
25: bool search(vector<vector<char> > &board,
26:      string& word,
27:      int* visited,
28:      int op, //0 up, 1 down, 2 left, 3 right
29:      int matchLen,
30:      int i, int j)
31: {
32:      if(matchLen == word.size()) return true;
33:      int row = board.size();
34:      int col = board[0].size();
35:      if(i+1<row && op!=0)
36:      {
37:        if(visited[(i+1)*col+j] ==0 &&
38:               board[i+1][j] == word[matchLen])
39:        {
40:          visited[(i+1)*col+j] =1;
41:          if(search(board, word,visited, 1, matchLen+1, i+1, j))
42:              return true;
43:          visited[(i+1)*col+j] =0;
44:        }
45:    }
```

```
46:    if(i-1>=0 && op!=1)
47:    {
48:      if(visited[(i-1)*col+j] ==0
49:         && board[i-1][j] == word[matchLen])
50:      {
51:        visited[(i-1)*col+j] =1;
52:        if(search(board, word, visited, 0, matchLen+1, i-1, j))
53:          return true;
54:        visited[(i-1)*col+j] =0;
55:      }
56:    }
57:    if(j+1<col && op!=2)
58:    {
59:      if(visited[i*col+j+1] ==0
60:         && board[i][j+1] == word[matchLen])
61:      {
62:        visited[i*col+j+1] =1;
63:        if(search(board, word,visited, 3, matchLen+1, i, j+1))
64:          return true;
65:        visited[i*col+j+1] =0;
66:      }
67:    }
68:    if(j-1>=0 && op!=3)
69:    {
70:      if(visited[i*col+j-1] ==0
71:         && board[i][j-1] == word[matchLen])
72:      {
73:        visited[i*col+j-1] =1;
74:        if(search(board, word, visited, 2, matchLen+1, i, j-1))
75:          return true;
76:        visited[i*col+j-1] =0;
77:      }
78:    }
79:    return false;
80: }
```

136. ZigZag Conversion

The string "PAYPALISHIRING" is written in a zigzag pattern on a given number of rows like this: (you may want to display this pattern in a fixed font for better legibility)

```
P   A   H   N
A P L S I I G
Y   I   R
```

And then read line by line: "PAHNAPLSIIGYIR"
Write the code that will take a string and make this conversion given a number of rows:

```
string convert(string text, int nRows);
```

convert("PAYPALISHIRING", 3) should return "PAHNAPLSIIGYIR".
» Solve this problem

[Thoughts]
Really a boring problem. It is actually a math problem. See example,
n=4
```
P     I     N
A   L S   I G
Y A   H R
P     I
```

N=5
```
P       H
A     S I
Y   I R
P L   I  G
A     N
```

if look at above examples, it's easy to see, for every layer, the index of the main element(red) is (j+1)*n +i, but for the inserted element(green) between two main elements is (j+1)*n −i

[Code]

```
1:  string convert(string s, int nRows) {
2:      if(nRows <= 1) return s;
3:      string result;
4:      if(s.size() ==0) return result;
5:      for(int i =0; i< nRows; i++)
6:      {
7:          for(int j =0, index =i; index < s.size();
8:              j++, index = (2*nRows-2)*j +i)
9:          {
10:             result.append(1, s[index]); //red element
11:             if(i ==0 || i == nRows-1)  //green element
12:             {
13:                 continue;
14:             }
15:             if(index+(nRows- i-1)*2 < s.size())
16:             {
17:                 result.append(1, s[index+(nRows- i-1)*2]);
18:             }
19:         }
20:     }
21:     return result;
22: }
23:
```

Appendix - CodingTMD's Reading List

Following reading list will help you to gain a basic knowledge of what happened in current industry and bring you a little sense about how to design a distributed system with certain principles.

Concurrency

[1].   In Search of an Understandable Consensus Algorithm. Diego Ongaro, John Ousterhout, 2013

[2].   A Simple Totally Ordered Broadcast Protocol. Benjamin Reed, Flavio P. Junqueira,2008

[3].   Paxos Made Live - An Engineering Perspective. Tushar Deepak Chandra, Robert Griesemer, Joshua Redstone, 2007

[4].   The Chubby Lock Service for Loosely-Coupled Distributed Systems. Mike Burrows, 2006

[5].   Paxos Made Simple. Leslie Lamport, 2001

[6].   Impossibility of Distributed Consensus with One Faulty Process. Michael Fischer, Nancy Lynch, Michael Patterson, 1985

[7].   The Byzantine Generals Problem. Leslie Lamport, 1982

[8].   An Algorithm for Concurrency Control and Recovery in Replicated Distributed Databases. PA Bernstein, N Goodman, 1984

[9].   Wait-Free Synchronization. M Herlihy…, 1991

[10].   ZooKeeper: Wait-free coordination for Internet-scale systems. P Hunt, M Konar, FP Junqueira, 2010

Consistency

[1]. Highly Available Transactions: Virtues and Limitations. Peter Bailis, Aaron Davidson, Alan Fekete, Ali Ghodsi, Joseph M. Hellerstein, Ion Stoica, 2013

[2]. Consistency Tradeoffs in Modern Distributed Database System Design. Daniel J. Abadi, 2012

[3]. CAP Twelve Years Later: How the "Rules" Have Changed.
Eric Brewer, 2012

[4]. Optimistic Replication. Yasushi Saito and Marc Shapiro,
2005

[5]. Brewer's Conjecture and the Feasibility of Consistent,
Available, Partition-Tolerant Web Services. Seth Gilbert,
Nancy Lynch, 2002

[6]. Harvest, Yield, and Scalable Tolerant Systems. Armando
Fox, Eric A. Brewer, 1999

[7]. Linearizability: A Correctness Condition for Concurrent
Objects. Maurice P. Herlihy, Jeannette M. Wing, 1990

[8]. Time, Clocks, and the Ordering of Events in a
Distributed System. Leslie Lamport, 1978

Conflict-free data structures

[1]. A Comprehensive Study of Convergent and
Commutative Replicated Data Types. Mark Shapiro,
Nuno Preguiça, Carlos Baquero, Marek Zawirski, 2011

[2]. A Commutative Replicated Data Type For Cooperative
Editing. Nuno Preguica, Joan Manuel Marques, Marc
Shapiro, Mihai Letia, 2009

[3]. CRDTs: Consistency without Concurrency Control. Mihai
Letia, Nuno Preguiça, Marc Shapiro, 2009

[4]. Conflict-free replicated data types. Marc Shapiro, Nuno
Preguiça, Carlos Baquero, Marek Zawirski, 2011

[5]. Designing a commutative replicated data type. Marc
Shapiro, Nuno Preguiça, 2007

Distributed programming

[1]. Logic and Lattices for Distributed Programming. Neil
Conway, William Marczak, Peter Alvaro, Joseph M.
Hellerstein, David Maier, 2012

[2]. Dedalus: Datalog in Time and Space. Peter Alvaro,
William R. Marczak, Neil Conway, Joseph M. Hellerstein,
David Maier, Russell Sears, 2011

[3]. MapReduce: Simplified Data Processing on Large Clusters. Jeffrey Dean, Sanjay Ghemawat, 2004
[4]. A Note On Distributed Computing. Samuel C. Kendall, Jim Waldo, Ann Wollrath, Geoff Wyant, 1994
[5]. An Overview of the Scala Programming Language. M Odersky, P Altherr, V Cremet, B Emir, S Man, 2004
[6]. Erlang. Joe Ar mstrong, 2010

Systems
Implemented and theoretical distributed systems.

[1]. A History of The Virtual Synchrony Replication Model. Ken Birman, 2010
[2]. Cassandra — A Decentralized Structured Storage System. Avinash Lakshman, Prashant Malik, 2009
[3]. Dynamo: Amazon's Highly Available Key-Value Store. Giuseppe DeCandia, Deniz Hastorun, Madan Jampani, Gunavardhan Kakulapati, Avinash Lakshman, Alex Pilchin, Swaminathan Sivasubramanian, Peter Vosshall and Werner Vogels, 2007
[4]. Stasis: Flexible Transactional Storage. Russell Sears, Eric Brewer, 2006
[5]. Bigtable: A Distributed Storage System for Structured Data. Fay Chang, Jeffrey Dean, Sanjay Ghemawat, Wilson C. Hsieh, Deborah A. Wallach, Mike Burrows, Tushar Chandra, Andrew Fikes, and Robert E. Gruber, 2006
[6]. The Google File System. Sanjay Ghemawat, Howard Gobioff, and Shun-Tak Leung, 2003
[7]. Lessons from Giant-Scale Services. Eric A. Brewer, 2001
[8]. Towards Robust Distributed Systems. Eric A. Brewer, 2000
[9]. Cluster-Based Scalable Network Services. Armando Fox, Steven D. Gribble, Yatin Chawathe, Eric A. Brewer, Paul Gauthier, 1997

[10]. The Process Group Approach to Reliable Distributed Computing. Ken Birman, 1993

[11]. Bitcoin: A Peer-to-Peer Electronic Cash System.

[12]. The Hadoop Distributed File System. Konstantin Shvachko, Hairong Kuang, Sanjay Radia, Robert Chansler, 2010

[13]. Hive – A Petabyte Scale Data Warehouse Using Hadoop. A Thusoo, JS Sarma, N Jain, Z Shao, 2010

[14]. Scalable Web Architecture and Distributed Systems. Kate Matsudaira,

[15]. Kafka: a Distributed Messaging System for Log Processing. J Kreps, N Narkhede, 2011

[16]. Storm: Distributed and fault-tolerant real-time computation. Nathan Marz, 2012

[17]. Spark: Cluster Computing withWorking Sets. M Zaharia, M Chowdhury, MJ Franklin…, 2010

[18]. Flat Datacenter Storage. EB Nightingale, J Elson, J Fan, OS Hofmann, J Howell…, 2012

[19]. Ananta: Cloud Scale Load Balancing. P Patel, D Bansal, L Yuan, A Murthy…, 2013

[20]. F1 - The Fault-Tolerant Distributed RDBMS Supporting Google's Ad Business. Jeff Shute, Stephan Ellner…, 2012

[21]. BigTable, Dynamo & Cassandra – A Review. A Kala Karun, S Surendran, 2012

[22]. Windows Azure Storage: A Highly Available Cloud Storage Service with Strong Consistency. B Calder, J Wang, A Ogus, N Nilakantan…, 2011

Reliability

[1]. The Dangers of Replication and a Solution. J Gray, P Helland, P O'Neil, D Shasha - ACM SIGMOD Record, 1996

Industry Implementation

[1]. Hadoop Architecture and its Usage at Facebook.
      Dhruba Borthakur, 2009
[2]. WEB SEARCH FOR A PLANET: THE GOOGLE CLUSTER
      ARCHITECTURE. LA Barroso, J Dean, U Holzle - Micro,
      Ieee, 2003
[3]. HDFS scalability: the limits to growth. Konstantin V.
      Shvachko, 2010
[4]. Autopilot: Automatic Data Center Management.
      Michael Isard, 2007
[5]. Storage Infrastructure behind Facebook Messages:
      Using HBase at Scale. AS Aiyer, M Bautin, GJ Chen, P
      Damania, 2012
[6]. Scaling Memcache at Facebook. R Nishtala, H Fugal, S
      Grimm, M Kwiatkowski, 2013
[7]. Finding a needle in Haystack: Facebook's photo storage.
      D Beaver, S Kumar, HC Li, J Sobel, P Vajge, 2010
[8]. Apache Hadoop Goes Realtime at Facebook. D
      Borthakur, J Gray, JS Sarma..., 2011
[9]. Data Warehousing and Analytics Infrastructure at
      Facebook. A Thusoo, Z Shao, S Anthony, D Borthakur...,
      2010
[10]. Large Scale Computing @ Linkedin. Bhupesh Bansal,
      2009
[11]. An Analysis of Facebook Photo Caching. Q Huang, K
      Birman, R van Renesse, W Lloyd..., 2013
[12]. The "Big Data" Ecosystem at LinkedIn. R Sumbaly, J
      Kreps, S Shah, 2013
[13]. Data Infrastructure at LinkedIn. A Auradkar, C Botev, S
      Das..., 2012

Language
[1]. Deep C (and C++) . Olve Maudal and Jon Jagger, 2011

Others

[1].   ColumnStores vs. RowStores: How Different Are They
         Really? DJ Abadi, SR Madden, N Hachem, 2008
[2].   Hadoop and its evolving ecosystem. J. Yates Monteith,
         John D. McGregor, and John E. Ingram
[3].   Orleans: Cloud Computing for Everyone. S Bykov, A
         Geller, G Kliot, JR Larus, R Pandya, 2011
[4].   Twitter Data Analytics. Shamanth Kumar, Fred
         Morstatter, Huan Liu, 2013
[5].   MapReduce is Good Enough? If All You Have is a
         Hammer, Throw Away Everything That's Not a Nail!
         Jimmy Lin, 2012

Data Mining
[1].   Data Mining with Big Data. X Wu, X Zhu, GQ Wu, W
         Ding, 2014
[2].   SAMOA: A Platform for Mining Big Data Streams. G De
         Francisci Morales , 2013
[3].   Mining Big Data: Current Status, and Forecast to the
         Future. W Fan, A Bifet, 2013
[4].   Scaling Big Data Mining Infrastructure: The Twitter
         Experience. J Lin, D Ryaboy, 2013

Books
[1]. Cloud Design Pattern.
[2]. Data Access For Highly scalable solutions.
[3]. Computer Architecture - A Quantitative Approach.
[4]. DISTRIBUTED SYSTEMS - Concepts and Design. Fifth
     Edition. George Coulouris
[5]. Beautiful Architecture. Diomidis Spinellis, Georgios
     Gousios etc
[6]. Mining Social Media: Tracking Content and Predicting
     Behavior. Manos Tsagkias
[7]. Seven Databases in Seven Weeks. Eric Redmond and
     Jim R. Wilson

17177308R10172

Made in the USA
San Bernardino, CA
04 December 2014